THE
WANDERING
TAOIST

THE WANDERING TAOIST

Deng Ming-Dao

Portraits by
Kwan Saihung

Diagrams by
Deng Ming-Dao

HarperSanFrancisco
A Division of HarperCollinsPublishers

FIRST HARPER & ROW PAPERBACK EDITION PUBLISHED IN 1986.

Designed by Deng Ming-Dao

Library of Congress Cataloging in Publication Data

Deng, Ming-Dao.
    THE WANDERING TAOIST.
    1 Kwan, Saihung. 2. Taoists—China—Biography.
I. Title
BL1940.K93D46   1983   299′.514′0924 [B]   82-48925
ISBN 0-06-250226-3 (pbk.)

---

91   92   93   94   95   96   CWI   16   15   14   13   12   11   10   9   8

To my mother and father

and to my Sifu

Contents

Acknowledgments

No ONE achieves anything in life on one's own, and I am deeply obligated to the many people who have supported me and taught me. Although it is impossible to name all of them, I would like to thank some of those who have helped me in the writing of this book.

My mother and father aided me in a wide variety of ways, from giving concrete advice to offering simple emotional encouragement, and I am grateful for their generosity and love.

My sisters and brother, Tyi, Ellora, and Lance, my classmates, Joan, Wes, Susan, Jim, and Ellen, and my friends Mark, Grier, Sue, and Monica, provided sympathetic understanding.

My supervisors, Adele, Pam, and Beth, went beyond the limits of obligation in giving me leave from work. Without their consent, I would not have had the opportunity to complete this book.

Uncertainty and doubt about my writing troubled me until I spoke with Elizabeth Lawrence Kalashnikoff. She gave me guidance and precious advice. Through her, I found the confidence to write.

Clayton Carlson, my publisher, had faith in an unknown author and an unusual body of material. I am very appreciative of his efforts to bring this work out.

Yvonne Eastman spent many hours typing a difficult manuscript for the sake of our good friendship, and constantly reassured me. Her efforts were a great contribution.

Finally, I must humbly thank my *Sifu*, my master, Kwan Saihung. If I had never met him, I would undoubtedly have made many more mistakes in my life. The unique experience of his tradition has made me a stronger, braver, and more vital man.

It is he who has brought me so far, and his efforts leave me hopelessly indebted to him.

I feel I can never truly repay any of these people for their unselfish support. I only hope that in helping others, perhaps partly through this book, I might in some small way honor their gifts to me.

Note on Romanization

IT IS DIFFICULT to romanize the Chinese words necessary for this book. Although it seems best to use the pinyin system adopted by the People's Republic of China, many terms are familiar to the general reading public from other systems. The only alternative seems to be to use the pinyin system for all cases except those where a different spelling would enhance ready recognition.

Foremost among those words are, of course, *Tao* and *Taoism*. Under the pinyin system, they would be romanized as *Dao* and *Daoism*. I have retained the previous form because it is in widespread use. I have also spelled Sifu's name Kwan Saihung rather than Guan Shihong, because this is the way he himself spells it. All other proper names and technical terms have been rendered in pinyin, however; although in a few cases I have parenthetically added the Wades-Giles version of a name to ensure recognition. Regardless of how names are romanized, all surnames precede given names; hence *Guan* has been used as the surname for other members of Saihung's family, except Ma Sixing (due to the fact that a Chinese woman keeps her own surname after marriage).

Readers should take special note of several terms used throughout the book. *Qi, qigong,* and *Taijiquan* are the pinyin spellings of *ch'i, ch'i kung,* and *Tai Chi Ch'üan,* words well known to those familiar with Taoism and Chinese martial arts.

Introduction

Until China was unwillingly wrenched into the twentieth century, it was a self-contained universe. Its thousands of galaxies were the precise concentric circles of hundreds of family generations. Its worlds were of mist-obscured peaks, lacquered and tiled pavilions, mud and wattle cottages. Smells of camphor, sandalwood, lotus, and blood; tastes of millet, honey, bitterness, and tears; sights of gold, pageantry, and lepers; sounds of birdsong, temple bells, and swords—the Chinese universe was filled with an endless succession of sensations. It doubled back on itself, yielded constantly multiplying dimensions. It embraced all paradoxes, juxtaposing sorcerers and astronomers, peasants and lords, courtesans and beggars, sages and thieves. Magnificence, extravagance, and opulence alternated with savagery, desperation, and wretchedness. Mythology coexisted with fact. Legend became reality. In China—so wide, so expansive, so infinite—all things existed, and to their extremes.

Universes exist in time, and time had nurtured the tangled structure of China, twisting its branches far away from each other. Time had made China's extremes possible. For all was measured by repetition, and by repetition China's universe expanded. The farmer drew water daily, tilled his fields daily; the jade carver worked his whole life, cutting the same stone daily; the sage meditated daily. This was time: repeat, repeat, repeat. Repeat until repetition became perseverance. Repeat until perseverance became Endurance.

For over five thousand years China evolved into a swirling, densely layered place where the extraordinary was no longer strange. It had soberly progressed in ways even madmen could not have imagined. But its riches, brilliance, and government could overcome neither human suffering nor the Tao. For tranquility and peace were lacking, and escape from the Tao impossible. China was a universe, but that universe was only a rock in the stream of Tao. The highest elements of Chinese culture failed to satisfy the truth that the sages in faraway mountain hermitages knew: renounce the world. Follow the Tao.

But, oh, the world's seductions! Its marvels! Its delights! One might still try to lose oneself in its wonders. Yet one could meet, seemingly by accident, a Taoist who might hurl one into realms supernatural even for the magic of everyday China. That happened centuries ago to Lu Dongbin, a young student who, on his way to take the imperial examinations, met a mysterious man at an inn. The man gave Lu a pillow to sleep on. Thereon Lu dreamed his entire life: a life that was to reach great heights of success and accomplishment only to end in misfortune and murder. On awakening, Lu Dongbin perceived the vanity of the world, joined the traveler, Han Zhongli the Taoist, and eventually became an Immortal.

The Taoist mystics followed this example, renounced the world and withdrew to the mysterious realms of gods, immortals, spirits, and demons. They roamed heaven and earth, following the Tao, until the moment that they could transcend the mortal plane. But they did not leave until their traditions were transmitted to others. Kwan Saihung was one of those who received the sacred knowledge, beginning with his entrance into the Huashan hermitage as a small boy. Sixty years later, his stories, told in another land where legend and reality do not meet, still echo the vital life of that distant mountaintop.

Kwan Saihung is a solitary Taoist ascetic, the only member of the Zhengyi-Huashan sect outside China. Presently over sixty years old, he has also been a martial artist, circus acrobat, Peking Opera performer (specializing in the role of the Monkey King), soldier, political science professor, and undersecretary to Zhou Enlai. Since leaving China twenty years ago, he has traveled the world over, supporting himself as a masseur, waiter, cook, bar bouncer, and martial arts teacher.

Outwardly, he is not the stereotyped ancient Chinese sage of movies and books. He does not look older than his forties, he dresses in American clothes, and, with his heavily muscled figure, he has an athletic appearance. His command of the English language and American colloquialisms is astounding. But this is merely an outer façade. Inwardly, he carries the traditions of his sect. His primary activity is the daily practice of physical body-purifying austerities and deep meditation. He has even retired from teaching martial arts in order to pursue a reclusive life of contemplation.

He is not in the United States to propagate religion. His wanderings have led him here. He isn't a missionary. Instead, he wants only to practice his art. Although he gives every appearance of being at ease in a foreign country, the contrasts between current U.S. life and the traditional Chinese way must sometimes be difficult for him. He occasionally speaks of feeling exiled, as if he were not only separated from his homeland but had stepped into a time warp as well. He realizes that China is an ocean away and has irrevocably changed by quantum proportions.

He carries the seeds of Taoism but walks on alien soil. Perhaps those seeds could sprout here. But they can't be planted until the tree that bears them is understood and accepted. In order to do this, we have to reverse the time warp, span the distance, and go back to early twentieth-century China—a land that might initially seem as alien to us as modern U.S. society must sometimes seem to Kwan.

Kwan Saihung was born to an aristocratic warrior clan before 1920, a volatile time of political instability and cultural decay. It had not even been a full decade since the Qing dynasty had fallen. Warlords, Europeans, Americans, Japanese, Nationalists, and Communists fought bitterly over the pieces of the shattered empire. The Chinese civilization, for centuries so confident in its national strength that it had proudly called itself the Middle Kingdom, had collapsed both from within and without. Internally, the weight of an ancient, calcified, feudal structure—one that could not adequately address the problems of famine, flood, disease, overpopulation, rebellious peasantry, clashing conservatives and modernists, and industrial social values—weakened China immeasurably. How much its institutions had failed became even more apparent when it faced the West. Commercial competition, opium trading, invasion, unequal treaties, colonization by avaricious Europeans, the ideological challenge of Christian missionaries, and Japan's annexation of Shandong province in 1919 were only a few cases where China failed to defend itself against foreign encroachment. It was not that the Chinese people lacked determination and courage. But struggles of resistance such as the Boxer Rebellion, Revolution of 1911, and the student strikes arose from old superstititions, beliefs, and outlooks; each was correspondingly undermined by its outmoded approach. The weaknesses were too great. China was racked by constant conflict and warfare.

Culturally, China was equally troubled. Political history may move rapidly, but social evolution is often slow. This was very true of the Chinese. They clung stubbornly to their old ways. Everyday reality remained strongly feudal in character, and these social structures, though decaying, survived through the 1949 revolution.

The land was agricultural. Architecture in the cities and villages remained unchanged: walls of wood, brick, and stucco; latticework windows; peaked tiled roofs. Transportation was archaic, the sight of a train an unusual occurrence. Horses, donkeys, and boats were only for a fortunate few. Most walked. There was little electricity outside the cities. People dressed in their traditional garments, which symbolized the rigid class system: rich furs and high-collared silk brocade for the nobility, coarse cotton for the peasantry. Many men still wore queues, and many women still had bound feet.

China was entirely different from other countries of the world. It was not an industrial society but had instead brought its culture to an unrivaled peak in a uniquely Chinese way. Having preserved its way of life through isolation, China at that time was more like a highly advanced medieval society. If it had any echoes in the West at all, they were not with the members of the then budding League of Nations, but with King Arthur's time—when there were still knights, sorcerers, kings, priests, and peasants. China still structured itself along the similar Confucian relations of emperor to subject, lord to peasant, husband to wife, parent to child. Society was stratified into imperial, aristocratic, civil, military, warrior, priestly, scholarly, merchant, and agricultural castes, with no opportunity to leave one's class.

Kwan Saihung's family situation mirrored the conflict between old and new China. His grandfather—clan head, imperial official, scholar, martial artist and respected elder of five provinces—was in continual conflict with Kwan's father—warlord militarist and modernist. It was against this background of social and familial flux that the young Kwan was sent to a hermitage on Huashan. The mountain, half-way between the two ancient capitals of Xian and Luoyang—an area that was the very cradle of Chinese civilization—was a sacred center of Taoist asceticism. It was there that Kwan entered his Taoist order.

Tao must be defined before Taoism can be explained, but this is a difficult task. Literally, the word *Tao* means "the Way," yet that word does not adequately designate all that lies within this complete statement of the ultimate reality. The word itself has existed since the beginning of the Chinese written language. However, unlike Western languages where a word is a narrowly defined intellectual concept, the Chinese word is a pictograph. A symbol. Thus, although the word *Tao* or "Way" symbolizes the ultimate, it is meant only to indicate. It does not encompass. The Tao is limitless. It is all that we can imagine and all that we cannot imagine. The Tao cannot be circumscribed by words and definitions. It cannot truly be discussed. It must be *perceived*.

Lao Tzu, the prominent Taoist sage who lived during the sixth century B.C., wrote in the *Tao Te Ching*,

> *There was something mysteriously formed,*
> *That existed before heaven and earth;*
> *Silent and void, dependent on nothing;*
> *Eternal;*
> *All pervading, unfailing.*
> *One may call it the mother of all under heaven.*
> *Its true name is unknown.*
> *Tao is the name we give it.*

We cannot name the Tao, only our narrow conception of it. The true, nameless, and limitless Tao is what is absolute.

By defining the absolute as a way, reality was seen as an ever flowing, ever changing continuum. The Way was not linear, but cyclical: the ancients observed that *change* in the universe—whether in the stars, planets, or seasons—was the underlying principle, and that it followed cycles of rotation, frequency, or expansion and contraction. The Way was not material: it was force, not matter. The Way was not a god or being: if there had been a "creator," the Way preceded such an entity. The Way, in its limitlessness, could rightfully be called *Wu Ji*: "Nothingness."

The Tao was best perceived in nature, not because nature was the Tao, but because nature perfectly mirrored the Tao in two fundamental ways. It existed solely in action—having no consciousness of itself—and, though it was always changing, remained in constant equilibrium.

Humanity, in the time long before recorded history, was part of the natural equilibrium and lived in harmony with the cosmic flow. There was no Tao*ism*. Since humanity was not separate from Tao, a doctrine was unnecessary. But the instant human beings in their vanity set themselves apart, they distanced themselves from the Way. Distinction and consciousness emerged. Methods then had to be invented by the sages to reintegrate humanity, to obliterate the consciousness of the human being as a separate entity, and to return to the equilibrium of the way. Civilization was the crystalization of human vanity. Taoism has therefore existed since the beginning of civilization.

Taoism's earliest known sages were three legendary Chinese emperors. The first was Fu Xi, 2800 B.C., who formulated divination and agriculture. The second was Shen Nung, 2700 B.C., who began herbology by experimentally ingesting herbs himself and noting the effects. The third was the Yellow Emperor, 2696–2598 B.C., who codified medicine, including surgery and acupuncture, in his *Classic of Internal Medicine*. Still used by Chinese physicians today, the book makes following the Tao its central theme and notes how medicine can return the ill to a state of health defined as complete balance with the Tao. The contributions of each of these three sages are all clear ways to return to the Tao.

In subsequent centuries, enlightened sages, or, immortals, gradually taught other aspects of the Tao. Eventually, these included contemplation of nature, meteorology, astronomy, divination, geomancy, astrology, sorcery, military strategy, medicine, philosophy, martial arts, ascetic austerities, painting, poetry (Li Po and Su Dongpo are two well-known examples), music, calligraphy, ritual, and meditation. The sages also left a large collection of scriptures, and the Taoist Canon grew to be hundreds of volumes. Most notable among those translated in the West are the *I Ching, Tao Te Ching,* and *Chuang Tzu.*

Taoism became a complex, pluralistic system in the forty centuries since its legendary beginnings. It is concerned with four major areas: the philosophical (*Lao Tzu* and *Chuang Tzu,* for example), the ritualistic (temple worship of countless gods and goddesses), the talismanic (sorcery and magic to ward off evil), and the ascetic (the tradition of gaining immortality or spiritual enlightenment through elixirs or meditation). This is simply a rough division; most Taoist sects combine the four in varying proportions. Almost all orders, for example, maintained public temples that both served their constituencies and brought financial support for more esoteric practices.

Early on, the quest for immortality became a fundamental Taoist activity. There is no ready explanation as to why it became such a deep concern. It may have been a simple primitive desire to avoid death, the logical extension of Taoist health practices, a part of the doctrine of reincarnation, or, according to some Taoists, an effort to return humanity to a time when all were actually immortal. But, whatever the reason, Taoists in search of immortality tried many methods of prolonging life. They experimented with alchemical elixirs, meditation, herbology, and numerous other methods. Some, in their fanaticism, gained exactly the opposite: they died from eating metals such as gold, tin, and lead, thinking such practices would lead to success.

The quest for immortality demanded utter devotion and was a contributing factor toward the reclusive life. Some became hermits, while others chose a life of wandering that followed the Tao. A distinction thus arose between those who traveled and those who remained in the temple. Those attached to a temple were *Tao Shi*. Those not attached were traveling renunciates interested only in spiritual goals; they were called *Tao Yin*. Similar to the Indian sadhus, these individuals seldom settled down. They were the wandering Taoists.

Taoism's long evolution naturally gave rise to a plethora of schools. In China, the culture was divided into northern and southern, and Taoism was no exception. Five great branches of Taoism eventually emerged, the first three, northern, and the last two, southern:

Jade Capital:	Maoshan, sorcery
Heavenly Pivot:	Lungmen and Huashan, asceticism
Pole Star:	Wudangshan, military arts, exorcism
Jade Prefecture:	Lunghushan, priestly
Spirit Cloud:	Lushan, priestly, some Buddhist influence

Huashan, though officially listed in the northern, Heavenly Pivot branch, in fact held itself separate from most of the doctrinal distinctions of the northern and southern schools. Calling itself the *Western School* (Huashan was the western peak of China's Five Sacred Mountains), it disassociated itself from the North-South competition and instead practiced internal alchemy. In brief, Huashan Taoists believed that enlightenment, spiritual liberation, transcendence of reincarnation, and attainment of immortality were possible only through purification of the body and mind through diet, exercise, herbal regimens, *qigong* (breath training), and meditation. Concurrently, the practitioner was also to gain mastery in the scholarly, martial, and liturgical arts.

Kwan Saihung entered the South Peak Temple at the age of nine. He eventually became the last of thirteen disciples under the Grand Master of Huashan, for Taoist practices could be transmitted only directly through the guidance of an accomplished master. How a young boy was led to a life of renunciation and how he preserved his legacy in spite of the turmoil of Chinese society in the early twentieth century are critical reminders that spirituality is possible even in the darkest of times. Understanding his struggles to nurture the Tao right into a different era, country, and culture, is an inspiration to save any possible portions of his tradition before he leaves the world for his final stage.

PART ONE

CHILDHOOD

ONE

The Taishan Festival

I N 1929, Kwan Saihung* accompanied his family on a pilgrimage up the steep slopes of Taishan. They were traveling to the Emerald Cloud Temple at the mountain's summit for the Festival of the Jade Emperor, a religious event that combined weeks of ritual and devotion with a carnival-like atmosphere in the temple courtyard. The Guan family, members of an immensely wealthy warrior clan, were devout patrons of Taoism who were completing a long and arduous pilgrimage of over five hundred miles from their home in Shaanxi Province to Shandong Province. They would be guests of the temple for a month.

The final ascent of Taishan, by means of sedan chairs, was slow. Taishan's towering precipices could not be scaled in a day. But the gradual climb, divided by overnight lodging in rustic inns situated in pine groves, provided an opportunity for final ablutions. All the inns served only vegetarian foods, and the cleansing of the taint of animal flesh and the opportunity for contemplation quieted the pilgrims' minds.

The mountain itself made complete their otherworldly state of mind. Taishan was the foremost of the Five Sacred Mountains of China. It rose steeply above Shandong Province's vast expanse, disdaining all the other mountain ranges, whose peaks were flooded by clouds so far below it. It had a heavenly magnitude, an air of imperial seclusion. Humanity was invisible from its summit, and in the cool and rarified air surrounding its high cliffs of rock, Taishan was the perfect place of solitude for the Jade Emperor.

* *Kwan* and *Guan* are variants of the same surname.

An emperor, whether celestial or mortal, was, for the Chinese, a personage never to be seen by common people. He was a mystery, a force, an inaccessible but dominating power. But on the annual occasion of the Festival, the Jade Emperor granted one exception to that rule and descended to his earthly abode to accept personally the supplications of his subjects.

Saihung, an energetic, mischievous, and curious nine-year-old boy, was less interested in the religious significance of the event than he was in simply having fun. His grandfather Guan Jiuyin, his grandmother Ma Sixing, and his aunt Guan Meihong understood this. They did not want to force things on Saihung but nevertheless felt that it was time for him to experience his first pilgrimage. It was with that in mind that the family faced the final approach to Taishan, the Eighteen-Twist Path.

The path was a narrow ribbon of 7,000 stone steps that followed the twisted crags of a huge cleft. Compared to the rugged granite cliffs, netted with tenacious shrubs and trees, the pathway seemed positively fragile. It was a man-made object, insignificant compared to nature, and appeared barely tolerated by the mountain. The adults were carried up in their sedan chairs, but Saihung, though he had the option of being carried on the back of a manservant, bounded up the stairs in excitement.

The early morning air was thin and cold, and Saihung was warmly dressed in a high-collared, fur-lined coat of mountain lion skin over a suit of heavy maroon cotton. The knicker pants buttoned at the knee over white leggings and both his shoes and money pouch were intricately embroidered silk. The shoes were felt-soled, with blue and white clouds decorating the sides and gaily colored appliquéd lion heads at the toes. The money pouch, barely visible at the hem of his coat, had a design of a frolicking lion. All of Saihung's clothing emphasized the masculine to enhance his personality and to ward off evil. Families were very concerned about such protections, and for good measure Saihung wore a tiger's tooth around his neck as a talisman.

Saihung at age nine

Two other items of clothing completed this outfit, and Saihung hated them both. Now that he was running up the steps, he had grown too warm. He first pulled off his hat. It also was of mountain lion skin, with flaps that covered the ears and two decorative lion's ears that stuck up at the crown. These protrusions were the one detail Saihung most disliked, and he took the opportunity to fling the cap away. He also removed the second item he hated, his mittens. These were, to his chagrin, impossible to dispose of. They had been securely sewn with silken cords to his coat sleeves. Still, with the hat gone and the mittens dangling, he finally felt free of encumbrance as he ran up the steps. His bobbing head, completely shaven except for a square patch of hair at the forehead, could be glimpsed as he darted among the other pilgrims.

The steps seemed endless. Saihung had stopped to rest at the side when his family's entourage caught up with him. The lead sedan chair, with its latticework windows, reduced his grandfather to a silhouetted presence. Evidently, however, his grandfather could see him perfectly well, for his deep voice soon came booming out from behind the latticework.

"Saihung! Where is your hat?"

Saihung looked up innocently. "I must have left it at the inn, Grandfather."

There was a patient sigh from within the chair. One of the servants brought the hat out. Saihung grimaced at him and was preparing to kick the man's shins when his grandfather called sharply to him. With a pout, Saihung put on the hat.

Once again running ahead of the procession, however, Saihung grinned. He knew he was his grandfather's favorite, and he knew that his grandfather, though firm, was also indulgent and forgiving.

When the family reached the temple gates, the abbot personally came out to meet them. The abbot was an old friend and had prepared one of the temple's pavilions for the Guan family's living quarters during their stay.

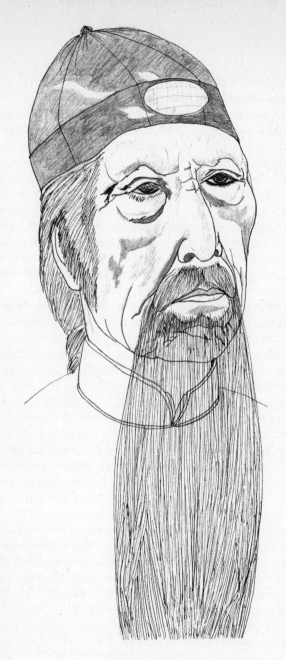

Guan Jiuyin

Guan Jiuyin was the first to descend from his chair. Already in his mid-seventies, he was nevertheless impressively large and muscular. Over six feet in height, his size alone would have set him apart from others. The richness of his dress and his obvious charisma completed his unusual image. His fur-lined burgundy tunic and pants, black brocade vest, black cap with its piece of apple-green jade, snow-white beard, and braided hair fittingly accentuated the placid but alert expression of a warrior.

Ma Sixing, a year younger and only a few inches shorter than her husband, was the next to greet the abbot. In spite of bound feet, she walked unaided. Her slender figure was covered by expensive brocades. Over her own fur-lined tunic and trousers, she wore a long apron and a cowl, both of which were hand-embroidered in a palette of bright colors and metallic thread. Roses, chrysanthemums, fuchsias, peonies, and irises formed a complex and dazzling pattern. Long and thick, combed away from her face and pinned with jeweled ornaments, her white hair was in a coiffure that emphasized her high cheekbones and the lunar complexion of her beautiful face. Her large almond-shaped eyes shone softly, like a doe's, but this gentle appearance masked an inner ferocity.

Charm and grace had not abandoned her in her old age, and many of the other women who glimpsed her during the festival must have envied her. But unlike these conventional beauties, she always displayed, in addition to silken sashes and jade bracelets, a long rawhide whip coiled over her left shoulder. This was her personal weapon.

Saihung's aunt, Guan Meihong, was plainer and darker than her mother. In her fifties, she was dressed in a blue velvet suit. Although her cowl and apron were also embroidered, she had simpler tastes, and usually dressed somberly. She had only recently unbound her feet and walking even with the help of a cane was painful.

When Saihung was introduced to the abbot, he dutifully gave his greetings, bowing deeply. But after he saw that the

Ma Sixing

adults had turned to conversation, he slipped through the temple gates.

The temple courtyard burst with a frenzy of activity in a setting of bright colors. Against a background of the temple's bronze-tiled roofs, polychromed eaves, ridgepoles, and worn red brick walls, thousands of hand-painted silk lanterns, pinwheels, and tiny bells swung above stalls, stages, and crowds of people. Musicians, acrobats, puppeteers, magicians, and musclemen were performing throughout the courtyard. Priests, dressed in patched gray robes, strolled among the people selling incense, talismans, and votive objects. Some gave advice, while others predicted people's fortunes. But the best of all, to Saihung, were the many food stands offering fresh, steaming vegetarian food and delightfully sweet candy.

Eating, for Saihung, was even more wonderful than getting into mischief, and he had a great appetite for both. Although he wanted to explore the entire festival, he could hardly refuse the temptation of fragrant food. He bought many different kinds of candies, some of which he ate on the spot, saving the others in his pockets. Only after he had found his favorite—miniature apples skewered and dipped in honey—did he go to the rest of the festival.

He squeezed his way through the dense forest of trousers and skirts to the center of the courtyard. On a high platform was a group of darkly dressed musicians performing from a large repertoire of operas, popular songs, and classical works. They had a good range of instruments, including the lute, harp, and violin, the flute and other reed instruments, and an arsenal of gongs, cymbals, and percussion instruments. Armed with this mighty array, the musicians were wholly unconcerned with the already roaring din of the festival. They played loudly and shrilly, finishing off each section of a song with wildly crashing cymbals and gongs to make themselves heard.

Whenever another group was ready to perform on another stage, its figures would cry out loudly like carnival hawkers,

promising great entertainment and unimaginable feats. Saihung was attracted by the announcement of a magician.

"Come! Come! Come! Uncles and Aunts! Sisters and Brothers! Elders and Children! Come! Come! Come! See amazing
things, magic to make the gods jealous, magic that will leave
you incredulous! Come! Come!"

Saihung rushed over to see a tall, dark man with arching
eyebrows, and eyes that glared exaggeratedly. Dressed in red
silk, he strolled forward haughtily to the stage edge, and without preliminaries, made silk scarves appear and disappear
from his hands; materialized fans, bowls, and vases from behind a small bouquet of flowers; and shot flames from his
sleeves. But he soon discarded the props disdainfully, as if to
say that those were mere parlor tricks. He addressed the
crowd.

"Elders, Uncles, Aunts, and Children. I have spent fifty
years as a magician. I've known immortals and priests, sorcerers and recluses. I have learned obscure secrets, but none so
amazing as mesmerism."

In short order he extracted a volunteer from the crowd—a
fat man with a pock-marked face who openly voiced his skep-
ticism. The magician focused his eyes on the man, who had
folded his arms in utter determination. The crowd was silent.
The man's arms slowly fell.

"You troublesome bumpkin!" cursed the magician. "You
really should have been born as—a chicken!" The man immediately began flapping absurdly about, jumping and pecking.
Everyone roared with laughter.

From another platform, loud cries announced another act.

"Hey! Hey! Come see the musclemen of Mongolia! Come see
great feats of strength!"

Saihung rushed over to see several brutish men, grinning
coarsely and grunting vulgarly. Poking at one another, they
burst into laughter as they joked among themselves. The larg-
est one came forward, dressed in heavy boots, white cotton
pants, and a red fur-lined vest over his bare torso. He flexed

his muscles, and his dark-skinned chest and arms inflated grotesquely.

He picked up an iron bar that no one in the audience could bend. He twisted it and straightened it. There was applause. The muscle man smiled in appreciation, showing broken yellow teeth. He held his hand up for silence. Walking over to a stack of bricks, he poised himself. With a gutteral cry, his head came smashing down, splitting the entire stack.

Saihung finished the last of his candy apples before the applause had ended. He debated with himself about what to do next. There were the acrobats, the puppet shows of the Monkey King, and the Romance of the Three Kingdoms, and there was still plenty more to eat. He was still deliberating when someone slapped his head. He spun about angrily, but his expression immediately changed when he saw the cane.

"So here you are, running away again!" said his aunt.

"Oh, Auntie, did you see the musclemen?"

"Saihung! Don't try to get out of it. You know you are not supposed to run about alone! Anyone can see you're a wealthy boy, a child from an aristocratic family. There are always bandits, some who even pose as priests, ready to kidnap boys just like you."

Saihung looked unconvinced.

"You'd better be good, Saihung," warned his Aunt. "Perhaps you aren't afraid of men with knives, but there are also demons!"

Saihung looked up immediately. He remembered tales his uncles back home had told him. His aunt shrewdly noticed his vulnerability.

"Yes, Saihung. They lurk around in shadows simply waiting for plump, naughty boys like you. When one comes along, they grab him, put him into a sack, and hang him upside down in their caves until they're ready to cook him in a big cauldron."

Saihung rushed immediately to her side, grateful that it was daytime and that there were few shadows. He took his aunt's hand. But he was not one to go docilely.

"Auntie," he said, looking up sadly. "I want to see the rest of the fair."

"There's time, Saihung. We'll be here many days."

"But I want to see it now."

"Your grandparents are wondering about you. We must go back, but you'll see more along the way."

"All right . . . but Auntie?"

"Yes?"

"I've not had anything to eat. Will you buy me something?"

TWO

A Chance Encounter

IN THE DAYS that followed, Sai-hung had time to explore the rest of the festival under his aunt's supervision. The temple became playground, theater, and restaurant for him and provided endless diversions. He met other children and became friends with them. Together, he and his new companions made up games, snacked, or looked at the many performances.

But the Taishan Festival was, after all, a religious event. Concurrent with all the festivities were daily rituals. The most important ritual was the Dance of the Big Dipper.

This ceremony was performed in stages over forty-nine days, in a specially consecrated courtyard. The purpose of the Dance was to integrate humanity with the cosmos, a fundamental Taoist concern, by calling to earth the gods who live in each of the Dipper's seven stars.

The stars were perfect worlds, and it was improbable that the gods would have voluntarily left their spheres to come to the human world. But the priests, by performing the dances and chanting invocations, could summon them, and the gods came to bestow blessings and provide divine aid. Only with the gods themselves present could the festival truly have spiritual power.

The priests fasted for seven days in order to purify themselves. They erected three poles and an altar before the main temple hall. Incense burners, red candles, flowers, oil lamps, and offerings were placed on the altar, and a large circle inscribed around it. Within the circumference of this circle were marked seven spots in the shape of the Big Dipper. Only then was the temple ready to receive the gods.

On the day Saihung went to see the ceremony, he saw the

abbot emerge from the temple in elaborate robes. Most of the priests who had been wandering in the festival dressed in worn, threadbare robes covered with patches, but the high priest was immaculately groomed. His long hair was put up beneath a black cloth hat, and he wore a robe embroidered with yin-yang symbols and hexagrams from the *I Ching*. The "windcatcher sleeves" were so long they hid his hands. He carried a datewood plaque inscribed with his own personal incantation, and a willow-wood sword. Walking gracefully on black velvet shoes with four-inch-thick soles, he performed devotions at the altar before stepping into the sacred circle.

Surrounding the perimeter of the circle, the pilgrims pressed in closely to view the dance, one of martial movements and swordplay. The abbot stood in turn on each of the spots that represented the stars. Holding the plaque before his face because mortals were unworthy to gaze at the gods, he chanted long invocations and called each god by name.

Saihung thought the dance looked like great fun. He dashed into the sacred circle and ran behind the abbot to imitate his rhythm and twisting steps. A murmur went up among the assembled devotees.

"Saihung!" his horrified aunt cried. She stepped as discreetly as she could into the circle. Leaning unsteadily on her cane and swaying on her tiny feet, she quickly pulled him back into the crowd.

"How could you do such a thing?" she scolded. "It's sacrilege to step into the circle. Try to behave yourself. Really, you are so troublesome, sometimes I wish the bandits would take you!"

Ignoring the stares and whispered comments from the onlookers, she turned to watch the ceremony again, gripping Saihung's hand tightly.

"Auntie, I can't see."

His aunt did not reply. He tried again in a tiny voice, not daring to anger her more. She did not turn toward him, yet her grip reminded him that he was to stay with her. Saihung was momentarily grave. Was his aunt really mad this time? Had she actually meant for the bandits to take him away?

After a while, her grip relaxed and she once more was pleasant and smiling. When she let go of him to put her cane in the hand that had been holding his, she reminded him not to stray. But no sooner had she again immersed herself in watching the dance, than Saihung had quietly slipped off.

A strong fragrance of sandalwood incense attracted his attention. He had smelled it constantly during his stay at the temple, yet today it seemed to be especially strong. He decided to trace the scent to its source.

Saihung came to the main temple hall, a massive structure with a sparkling bronze-tiled roof nearly three stories above the courtyard. Saihung could see the multicolored eaves carved painstakingly with dragons, phoenixes, and other motifs. Golden calligraphy on dark wood plaques and red lacquered pillars framed the entrance to a cool, dark interior. Clouds of incense drifted languidly toward him.

Saihung went up the steep stone steps, pausing just at the threshold. It was so dark inside. He suspected that this might be the ideal environment for demons who ate little boys. He looked around carefully. Saihung had no idea what demons might actually look like, but since he saw only a few pilgrims he soon ventured in.

He found his way to the center of the hall to see within a high, gilded altar the life-sized figure of the Jade Emperor flanked on the left by the Queen Mother and on the right by the Princess of the Azure Clouds. The three sat behind a large, ornately carved teakwood altar table set with all the necessary objects of worship. A large urn holding incense, candles, oil lamps, porcelain vases filled with flowers, vessels of rice, tea, wine, fruit, sweets, and five dishes of herbs representing black, red, yellow, green, and white—the colors of the Five Elements and the Five Directions—meant that all under heaven was being offered to the gods. It was in this spirit of reverence that each pilgrim worshipped at the altar, placing incense sticks in the large urn and kneeling down on prayer cushions before each figure.

Not one to be left out, Saihung walked up to the altar and knelt down.

He looked up directly at the Jade Emperor, who was dressed in ceremonial robes of yellow silk embroidered with imperial dragons. The headdress was a flat board set horizontally on a hat from which thirteen strings of beads hung in front and behind his head. The Jade Emperor was seated on a tiger skin and held the imperial book of etiquette. His hands and face had been modeled perfectly of porcelain and his hair and beard were real hair. The artistry was flawless, and as Saihung met the Jade Emperor's benevolent gaze he completely forgot that the Emperor was a statue.

The Jade Emperor was the highest god of the Taoist pantheon, presiding over all other gods and the whole universe. Living in heaven in a grand palace, surrounded by ministers, officials, and his family, he decided all the affairs of the cosmos and, if necessary, commanded the heavenly armies to battle evil. Unlike other gods, his figure or image was not permitted to be placed in households. That would have been sacrilege. Instead, one had to make a pilgrimage to his temple in order to present a petition.

Saihung bowed low in front of the Jade Emperor before moving to the Queen Mother. Her face had rosy cheeks and red lips, and her hair was pinned with precious jewelry. She presided over banquets in heaven where the gods ate the peaches of immortality from her own orchards. Each peach took 3,000 years to ripen, and a single bite prolonged a life by 10,000 years.

Saihung then bowed to the Princess of the Azure Clouds. A daughter of the Jade Emperor, the Princess sat clothed in lustrous silken robes and wore a headpiece representing three birds with outstretched wings. She was a goddess who protected women and children, and women who desired children came to pray to her.

Whether they came with personal desires for healing, a good harvest, or a new child, all the worshippers had made their way up the steep face of Taishan to pray here. Only by presenting their needs and offerings directly could the pilgrims be assured of a response. Although Saihung had no immediate request, he cheerfully completed his imitation prayers among the pious gathering.

He began to take his leave of the altar when he noticed another grouping of figures. The central one appeared to be a tall Taoist elder with a kindly, bearded face, silvery hair combed up into a topknot held with a single pin, and a simple black robe over pristine white garments. Behind him were two figures who seemed to be young Taoist acolytes. Dressed in gray robes, black hair also set up in topknots, their beardless faces were calm and peaceful.

Saihung moved over to the group of figures, knelt down, and bowed so low that his forehead touched the ground.

He was startled by soft, amused laughter. Saihung straightened up instantly and looked around. He saw only the shadows of the pilgrims before the altar. The laughter came again. Saihung turned to face the figures. Reddening in embarrassment, he quickly jumped up to kick the old man for having tricked him. The two acolytes came forward to restrain him. Saihung struggled furiously and kicked them repeatedly.

The scene was unnoticed by the worshippers until there was a frantic scream from the doorway. Saihung's aunt, fearing that Saihung was being kidnapped, rushed across the temple hall. It was immaterial to her that it appeared to be a Taoist priest and his two acolytes. Renegade priests frequently descended from the mountains to kidnap children for ransom or slavery.

"Help! Police! Police!" she cried as she wrestled Saihung away. She turned angrily toward the priest and raised her cane to strike him.

The old priest only laughed merrily. He gently raised his

The Grand Master of Huashan

long, flowing sleeve and passed it before her face. She was instantly immobilized and fell into a trance.

The priest smiled and turned to Saihung, who stared back in bewilderment. He was unsure whether the man was a festival magician, a demon, a bandit, or truly a priest. Saihung found himself as motionless as his aunt—yet he was still conscious. His mind went blank of its speculations. Time seemed to lose its ability to arbitrate events. A communication, a mystery, passed between the two of them, and for however long that moment lasted nothing else existed. Saihung felt something deep, searing, and silent.

Saihung slowly became aware of the temple hall. In the flickering yellow candlelight, he saw the color return to his aunt's face. She snapped out of her trance as if there had been no intervening time. Seizing Saihung's hand, she ran from the temple.

When Saihung and his aunt arrived, Guan Jiuyin and Ma Sixing were sitting in one of the side pavilions drinking tea. Saihung's aunt readily recognized her mother's upright and slender figure and her father's imposing posture, but she also saw that her parents were chatting with guests. She was alarmed. It was the same priest and his acolytes.

"Meihong," said Guan Jiuyin as his daughter came up uncertainly. "We've heard all about it. There's been a misunderstanding. This is my friend and spiritual teacher, the Grand Master of Huashan in Shaanxi Province." He turned to the priest. "*Da Shi* [Great Master], I apologize if she has offended you."

Meihung instantly knelt down, but the priest raised her upward again.

"It's only a trivial incident, after all," he laughed. He turned to Saihung and spent a long time looking at him. The look was thoughtful, and no one dared to interrupt.

"Jiuyin."

"Yes, *Da Shi*."

"This is your grandson."

"Yes, *Da Shi.*"

"There is a blue star on his forehead. This marks him as someone special."

Saihung said nothing. He could understand neither the conversation nor his grandfather's unusual deference to the priest, but he was fascinated by the Grand Master's open smile and kind eyes.

The family waited quietly for the Grand Master to continue.

"His spirit did not need to return to this dusty world," said the Grand Master after many minutes. "He came willingly. But those who volunteer to return are given a task. If he is to fulfill his mission, he will need long training."

"*Da Shi,*" said Guan Jiuyin, "Would you undertake his training?"

The Grand Master looked up. His clear, bright eyes caught the brilliant afternoon sun and mirrored it perfectly. "Perhaps. Perhaps," said the Grand Master slowly. "But I retired from the world years ago, and am a renunciate. It would be difficult for me to take a student now, especially one who is so young. So very, very young."

Saihung rose before dawn the next morning to accompany his grandparents to a scenic spot on Taishan, the Sun-Observing Peak. This vista point was famous for being the best place to watch the sunrise.

Shandong Province was over-layered with darkness and clouds. Only gradually were the crests of the turbulent, swirling clouds lit by pale light. Soon that light reddened and set streaks of clouds blazing as the intensely bright disc of the sun burned away the night.

Saihung thought over all the events of the festival. He thought of the pageantry, the ritual, the Grand Master. He turned over in his mind all the rich images of the Taishan Festival, and they became fused in the flame of the dawning sun.

THREE

The Guan Family Mansion

T HE GUAN FAMILY MANSION, located in Shaanxi Province, was the center for a clan of sixty members. Situated at the base of a mountain and surrounded by 2,000 family-owned acres of forest and farmland, the mansion combined artistic landscaping with classical Chinese architecture. Its conglomeration of many separate buildings was protected by a high wall that made it a virtual fortress.

This castle reflected the Guan family's martial class, but it was not at all a dull or grim environment. In addition to being a family of warriors, the Guan family also embraced the tastes of statesmen, scholars, and artists. The castle was a sanctuary, a retreat of quiet, tree-shaded gardens with trickling streams and blossoming flowers. It was a place of luxurious handcrafted pavilions of wood and tile, bronze and gold, and of living quarters embellished by delicate latticework windows, their interiors rich with masterpiece furnishings and precious antiques.

Over four generations old and already imbued with history, the mansion complex was in an eccentric shape: it snaked around the base of the mountain in an undulating configuration. Aside from its strategic advantage of exposing only one wall with a single steel-studded gate to defend, the shape of the Guan family mansion reflected the planning of Taoist geomancy. The Guan patriarch who had established the estate had commissioned a Taoist priest to determine its best location and physical shape. No traditional Chinese ever built a home without a geomancer to calculate the complicated cross influences of location and orientation in relation to the cosmic forces of wind, water, earth, and destiny. Each builder endeavored to integrate his family harmoniously with the universe and, by following the flow of natural forces, to preserve his clan and make it prosperous. The Taoist who had laid the plans for the Guans had decreed that the mountainside was the most propitious location and the dragon form the ideal groundplan.

Thus it came about that the sixty family members and one hundred servants lived in a dragon-shaped citadel, with mountain cascades flowing through the estate and expansive rooflines arching to the sky. The head of the dragon—practically a separate fortress in itself—housed the current patriarch, Guan Jiuyin, and his family. The majority of the clan lived in the tail, with the servants, stables, classrooms, and martial training halls in the back and belly. The many rooftops had been constructed in such a way that from a short distance an observer could see a seemingly unbroken expanse of green tiles. These represented the dragon's scales. But with their green color, unique arrangements, and camouflage of trees, the rooftops made the Guan family mansion almost undetectable from a long distance.

Guan Jiuyin had retreated to this enclosed and self-contained world when the Qing dynasty had fallen in 1911. Once minister of education under the Empress Dowager, a scholar, statesman, respected elder in five provinces, and a master martial artist, Guan Jiuyin now sought solitude. He had hoped to spend his time in the pursuit of refined arts, for he enjoyed painting, poetry, and the study of Taoism. But he was the patriarch of a rich, powerful, aristocratic clan, and he found no rest from the outside world. Even within the mansion, Guan Jiuyin was besieged by attackers, faced personal responsibilities, and could not be insulated from China's social turmoil.

The mansion was attacked periodically by a wide variety of bandits, rivals, and would-be assassins. China in the 1920s was still chaotic and lawless. Large groups of bandits regularly raided villages and the estates of the wealthy. That was one of the reasons that almost all the members of the Guan family and their servants were trained in martial skills—to fight off criminals who themselves were expert fighters. Guns were not yet in wide usage, and personal proficiency still determined survival.

Rivalry between powerful leaders and clans was also common then, and what could not be settled any other way was perpetrated by intrigue. Although Guan Jiuyin had retired, he had been an outspoken advocate during his public life, and many still harbored anger toward him. Whenever two clans came into competition over wealth, power, or prestige, assassination was a common means of gaining dominance.

The Guan family also had rivals in a more uncommon way. As a warrior family, they were members of China's diverse and deep martial underworld. The martial underworld had its own rules and social codes, and one of these was the code of personal challenge. Members of the underworld frequently challenged one another to determine who was superior in skill and therefore rank. The more prestigious one's defeated opponent was, the greater the victory, and a clan patriarch such as Guan Jiuyin was a favorite target.

But Guan Jiuyin found China's social turmoil more disturbing than any physical assault. There were guards and servants who could fight, and he was still confident in his own skill, for he remained in constant readiness. All those physical attacks were to him simple efforts at outright destruction, which could be fended off. But the domestic social decay, the encroachment of modernization, the imperialistic invasion by the West, the civil war between the Nationalists and Communists, the rampages of the warlords, and the shifting in the values of the young presented dilemmas too important to ignore, too complex for individual solution.

He felt even most of those problems could be closed out by the mansion walls except the last, and there the walls were breached by the clan's own children. Foremost among those whose values conflicted with Guan Jiuyin was his son and Saihung's father, Guan Wanhong.

Guan Wanhong was a man entirely different from his father's cultured character. Wanhong, a fierce-tempered, ambitious, and ruthless general in warlord and Nationalist armies, wanted only wealth, prestige, and political power. Although he had received a classical, almost scholarly education, he was wholly uninterested in the traditional poetry and painting his father collected so devotedly. His one goal was to be a success in the modern world, and he had entered the military both because it suited his temperament and because he perceived it to be the swiftest possible means to rise to prominence.

Guan Jiuyin had frowned on Wanhong's decision to enter the military, though he himself was a martial artist. By Chinese standards, to be a martial artist and to be a soldier were not necessarily compatible. A martial artist was not only concerned with the self-perfection of one's physical skill, but was also concerned with justice, and, like a medieval European knight errant, championed the causes of the weak, poor, and defenseless. His only concern was to attain the highest possible level in the art, to fight for morality, to achieve the heroic. But a soldier did not act in this standard, for he was concerned not with morality, but with slaughter. He did not seek opponents qualified to compete with him, but indiscriminately destroyed all who opposed him. He was not an individual fighting for his honorable principle, but a tool to be manipulated by more powerful commanders. A soldier, to Guan Jiuyin, was a mercenary, a dupe, a hack, a butcher.

Father and son had argued for years, and the strain in their relationship became more and more pronounced. The two could scarcely meet without arguing. Before long, the strain was reflected even in the physical arrangement of the Guan family mansion: Guan Jiuyin exiled Wanhong and his family to separate houses and gardens away from his own and forbade Wanhong ever to wear a uniform or bring firearms into his presence. It was a continual struggle between old and new, between the classical and contemporary. For the moment, Wanhong was still subordinate. Guan Jiuyin was the clan patriarch who still held authority over him, and Wanhong always appeared before his father dressed in Chinese clothing.

But the world that Wanhong represented progressively eroded, however slowly, the old Chinese ideals.

Saihung was caught in the conflict between the two men. Wanhong wanted to raise Saihung in his own image, and Saihung's mother, though an art and music teacher, agreed with her husband. Together they wanted Saihung to have a scholarly education but to succeed in the world by entering military life. They began to pressure Saihung, as early as the age of four, to further their ambitions. The pressure became too great; Saihung was a rebellious child, eventually pronounced by his parents to be too obstinate and difficult.

In actuality, Saihung was more attracted by his grandfather's lifestyle. Guan Jiuyin noticed this. When Saihung one night suffered a ferocious beating by his drunken father, Guan Jiuyin took advantage of the opportunity. As the patriarch, the supreme familial authority, Guan Jiuyin took Saihung away from Wanhong and brought him to live in his own quarters. From that moment on, although he frequently returned to his father's pavilions to visit and play, Saihung stayed with his grandfather, and Guan Jiuyin assumed primary responsibility for Saihung's upbringing from the age of seven.

FOUR

The Mischievous Student

SAIHUNG, isn't it time you were with your tutor?"

Saihung froze instantly where he stood behind the rock arrangement. He turned to look back at Flying Cloud, the twelve-year-old retained by the family as Saihung's companion and playmate, who was hiding with him. Flying Cloud returned his own look of surprise. How could the patriarch see them?

Seeing no other alternative, Saihung jumped out. His grandfather was not even looking in his direction, but was strolling down the courtyard holding up a mynah bird in a bamboo cage. Guan Jiuyin had two exquisitely black-feathered mynahs, and like many Chinese gentlemen, took them on morning strolls to give them fresh air and to let them learn the songs of wild birds. Unfortunately, the mynah's favorite words were "I'm hungry! I'm hungry!"

Guan Jiuyin paused momentarily, turning his face toward Saihung. Saihung saw the aquiline profile, the silvery queue, one hand holding the cage up high, the other loosely curled behind his back. Guan Jiuyin's hands were one of his trademarks. Strong, heavy, thick-fingered, they had nails shaped like talons. They were the hands of an eagle-claw martial artist.

"Saihung, go to your tutor," said Guan Jiuyin firmly.

"Yes, Grandfather."

"And Flying Cloud . . . "

"Yes, Great Lord?"

"See that he goes now."

Saihung's tutor, a thin elderly man, welcomed his pupil enthusiastically. The prospect of once again studying the classics he cherished so dearly excited him. Unfortunately, neither the lessons nor the tutor inspired Saihung. Old Tutor was simply not the kind of man Saihung looked up to. Compared to the other men of the clan—most of whom were warriors, not scholars—Old Tutor seemed to have transcended physicality. His already minimal body seemed to exist purely as a frame for layers of clothing and as a support for a head.

Old Tutor had a sallow, wrinkled face with such thin flesh that many details of his skull bone were clearly evident. His thinning, gray queue and inadequate beard dangled lifelessly. His most energetic gesture was to open his eyes as wide as possible, all the while desperately trying to stabilize the wire-rimmed glasses that seemed incapable of finding equilibrium on his bridgeless nose.

Monotonous regularity marked each morning. The program consistently began with recitation, followed by written exercises and calligraphy lessons. Whether spoken or written, the sole source of his teaching was the basic Confucian classic, *The Four Books*. Although Saihung was young, the classics could not be compromised for the sake of children's understanding. The children had to accommodate themselves to the classics. Nevertheless, the tutor chose simpler passages, always emphasizing the Confucian virtues of self-cultivation, proper social and familial order, moral and ethical conduct, and, most importantly, filial piety.

These lessons, aside from their irksome dullness, were the object of Saihung's inward scorn. The Paragons of Filial Piety were children who seemed so lacking in independence that Saihung would have discounted them all. One lesson, for example, celebrated a small boy who noticed that though his parents had mosquito netting, they were still bitten every night. In order to prevent this, the boy preceded his parents into the bedroom, offering the mosquitoes his own body. He killed some, but the majority gorged themselves on his blood until they were too satiated to attack his parents. Through the boy's sacrifice, the parents were able to sleep well. Saihung, however, found the whole idea idiotic and therefore could not imagine himself as a filial son. Fortunately for Confucianism and, unconsciously, for Saihung, his grandparents' integration of Confucian values, rather than specific details from the tutor's lessons, was responsible for shaping his behavior as he grew.

Compared to the lectures and recitations, Saihung found his writing sessions more interesting. Although the classics were once again the subject, to be copied repeatedly in order to assure retention, Saihung thought of writing more as drawing. Guiding the ink-soaked brush was a graphic adventure.

Patiently, Old Tutor taught him to hold his brush perpendicular, with the palm cupped so deeply that a walnut could fit in the space. The brush was first charged by drawing it through the ink and pointing the tip on the inkstone. Then the character was built up stroke by stroke, each mark following a set order, in a definite place and with proper proportion. Constancy of motion was critical. Brushing too quickly caused the bristles to drag dryly, while too slow a stroke made the delicate mulberry paper swell with blurs.

During his writing lessons, Saihung could depend on one familiar event. Old Tutor would often fall asleep. Today, as dependably as ever, Old Tutor sat gazing at the ceiling, his mind fixed on some obscure thought. Before long, scholarly musings gave way to slumber.

Saihung finished the last ideograph, a complicated structure of twenty-four strokes. Each time that the Old Tutor fell asleep, Saihung faced a dilemma of continuing his lessons or playing. It was a tribute to the Confucian system that most of the time he chose to finish his lessons and diplomatically awaken his tutor with a cough. But today he saw a tantalizing possibility. The more he contemplated it, the more appealing it grew. Possibility quickly changed to probability.

He carefully crept behind the unmoving figure. The scholar's queue dangled enticingly. Grasping it gently, Saihung knotted it to the chair.

He went to the door and looked outside. Flying Cloud was waiting patiently.

"Old Tutor! Old Tutor!" Saihung called from the doorway.

There was no response.

"He must really be visiting the sages," Saihung whispered to his companion. He turned back, and cupping his hands to his mouth, screamed out to his tutor once more.

The Old Tutor's tired eyes fluttered hesitantly. Seeing that his student's chair was empty, they blinked in puzzlement.

"Old Tutor!"

Saihung and Flying Cloud raced into the garden as they heard the tutor's outraged squawk.

"Young Lord," said Flying Cloud, after their giggling had stopped. "Aren't you afraid of punishment? He's sure to tell the Matriarch."

Saihung grinned naughtily as he reached into his pocket for some candy. "As long as I stay near Grandfather, she won't hit me."

Afternoons were devoted to playing and exploring the fascinations of the mansion. In quick order, the two boys had played games of tag, teased the maids, played hide-and-seek in the clan chapel—coming dangerously close to knocking over both the porcelain statute of Guan Gong (Kuan Kung), the God of War, and the prayer tablets of ancestors—fed Saihung's pet panda cub, and looked at Ma Sixing's black horse with the white mane. Laughing and out of breath, they found themselves sitting on the stone steps of Ma Sixing's training hall.

"What are they doing in there?" asked Saihung.

"The Matriarch is training the women."

"Let's take a look. Maybe we can pick up some techniques."

Flying Cloud tried to resist. It was his duty to keep Saihung out of trouble. Mustering as lofty a Confucian expression as he could, he said with dignity, "It is not allowed, Young Lord."

Saihung scrutinized his companion. He imagined Flying Cloud as a dried-up old scholar with glasses and beard.

"The Matriarch permits no visiting," intoned Flying Cloud somberly. "Remember propriety, Young Lord."

Saihung laughed. "Yes, but what if the Matriarch didn't know?"

Flying Cloud's expression changed from Confucian severity to boyish shock. "Young Lord!"

Saihung smiled. He had cracked part of the scholarly façade. But he could still imagine a wispy beard on Flying Cloud.

"We'll climb up on the roof," said Saihung mischievously.

"Young Lord!"

There goes the beard, thought Saihung with delight. Now he's just a boy again.

Since the courtyard doors were locked and there was frosted glass behind the latticework window, the only way to sneak a peek was to climb up onto the ridgepole and remove some of the unmortared roof tiles. Saihung began climbing a nearby tree, and Flying Cloud, caught in a conflict between his better judgment and his duty to follow Saihung everywhere, climbed with him. Stepping carefully across the roof of a lower gallery, they climbed onto the main roof. The tiles were smooth and set at a steep angle, but by clinging to the cornerline of the rooftop they inched on to the flat ridgepole. Flying Cloud was trembling. Saihung was oblivious to the height.

They crawled to the center and, lying on their stomachs, removed some of the tiling. Ma Sixing was in clear view, supervising a group of sparring women.

Ma Sixing, the daughter of a Qing dynasty prime minister, had studied martial arts from a Buddhist nun on Emieshan in Sichuan Province. Throughout Chinese history, monks and nuns living on isolated mountaintops had needed self-defense against bandits and animals and, adding metaphysical knowledge to boxing forms, had developed sophisticated fighting techniques. They added long periods of practice time to that legacy, passed it on within their sects and, on rare occasions, to secular pupils. Ma Sixing had lived in the nun's temple, mastering not only freehand fighting but *qinna* (seizing and bone locking), *qinggong* (the ability to lighten the body at will for jumping and acrobatics), and weapons as well.

Her art had been developed by women for women. Taking into account the vulnerabilities and limited strengths of women, the nuns had devised unique forms of training internal energy. They evolved a sophisticated internal alchemy rooted in female chemistry. Trained in practices forbidden ever to be seen by men, a woman could fearlessly face any attacker with ferocious strength and skill.

Ma Sixing's weapons had a feminine character, but they were nevertheless formidable. Chief among these was her whip, made of twenty-three sections of braided rawhide. Each section was capped with a steel sphere and chainlinked to the next section. Another weapon was the sash that bound her waist. It was interwoven with steel threading and had a row of steel balls dangling at each end. The sash was versatile, always available, and could be used for strangling or whipping. Finally, throwing darts were disguised as her hair ornaments, and short, slim daggers were concealed in her sleeves.

Saihung recognized most of the students as maids. On a few occasions, he remembered hearing how the women servants had killed intruders in the night by quietly strangling them with steel-threaded sashes. Now he could see the full range of their training methods, from shadowboxing and sparring to striking sandbags and wooden dummies.

In the center of the hall were 108 pyramids of delicate porcelain rice bowls on which the women could stand. Each pyramid was made of five bowls, four placed upside down in a square shape on the floor and a fifth overturned bowl on top. The 108 stacks were arranged one step apart and formed a plum blossom pattern.

Two women were fighting with their feet on the pyramids. By stepping only on the tiny bowls, they strengthened their legs, perfected their balance, and trained in *qinggong* as they stepped or jumped from stack to stack. All the while they were striking and kicking, aiming especially for delicate pressure points. So sure was their footing that they neither displaced nor broke the fragile pyramids.

In spite of their expertise, the women still made mistakes. When this happened, Ma Sixing, who sat attentively in a chair at the head of the hall, displayed her own ability with *qing-gong*. Wielding a split bamboo stick, she leapt out of her chair, covering over twenty feet with a gliding jump, to mete out her punishment.

After some time of practice, the women were dismissed. Saihung looked eagerly down, expecting to see his grandmother's own practice. But Ma Sixing went into another room and closed the door behind her. Her personal practice was a secret from everyone.

That evening, Saihung sat quietly in the shadows of his grandfather's pavilion. Twilight had shimmered for only a moment before it had plunged into deep indigo, and the Milky Way was a fine spray around the waxing moon. The temperature of the air had cooled, and a faint breeze set orange maple leaves dancing over the dark, rippling pond.

On a tiny island, framed by lotus leaves, stood a small gazebo. It had a peaked tile roof, red pillars, and patterned cut-out windows on each side. The glow of light from the main buildings barely defined its contours, but the interior of the gazebo was lit by a solitary candle.

In its flickering light, Saihung saw his grandmother seated before her Chinese harp. In the space just big enough for her, she seemed like a fairytale image. She had released her uncut hair and it formed a snowy mantle down her back. Her silken gown, embroidered with tortoises and autumn leaves against a wisteria-colored background, echoed her surroundings. Sitting completely still, she relaxed, abandoning daily responsibilities, letting moments slip luxuriously by. Then her fingers, pale as sculpted ivory, selected a string.

She felt each string against her fingertips and noticed the subtle gradations of their diameters. She plucked the first tone. It vibrated gently. Soon the courtyard reverberated with her song. Some staccato passages pierced like dagger thrusts, others spread out wide and low over the pond, and occasionally a single ending note trembled like a sob.

Guan Jiuyin sat inside the pavilion, reading a slim volume of poetry by Su Dongpo. The rhythm of the harp accorded naturally with the meter of the poetry. He was at peace. No matter what happened during the day, the cool evenings afforded him solitude. Sometimes he composed poetry with Ma Sixing. At other times he practiced painting, calligraphy, martial arts, or read. But whatever the activity, he treasured these intimate moments, sharing only with his wife and Saihung the time when nature renewed the pulse of life.

"Grandfather?"

Guan Jiuyin looked at Saihung, who was sitting beside him. Saihung turned from the window. "Tell me a story, Grandfather."

"What story would you like to hear?"

Saihung looked at his grandfather's hands, thought of the times he had seen his grandfather practicing his self-created spear style, the Blood Spear, and promptly replied, "I'd like to hear more about Bai Mei."

Guan Jiuyin assented with a laugh and carefully laid his book down.

"Now listen carefully, Saihung. The last time we talked, I had just begun telling you about Bai Mei—the White Eyebrow priest. He was a great Taoist, so accomplished in internal alchemy that neither punches nor weapons damaged any part of his body. He also created his own martial style—unique because it was patterned neither on a philosophical idea nor on imitating animals: it was a form based on human movements.

"Bai Mei was a true renunciate but the world pursued him. No matter where he went, society chased him. Two separate groups sought him out because of his martial abilities, the rulers of the Qing dynasty, and the rebels who sought to overthrow them. They all realized that anyone who had Bai Mei on their side and mastered his art would have a distinct advantage. Each side came to force him to join them or else to kill him.

"Bai Mei was not interested in either side and with pride and confidence finally responded to the threats by attacking the Forbidden City itself. Leading seventy-two of his disciples, he stormed into the palace. But it was a disaster. The fore-warned imperial troops ambushed and trapped them.

"The Emperor came out and mocked them. But he was shrewd: he would spare them, if they joined him. There was no choice. Bai Mei became the Emperor's personal guard.

"The Emperor was not the least bit afraid of being assassi-nated. He himself was a great martial artist, and he used a complex system that played one man against another. The Em-peror had men even greater than Bai Mei in his court. Mysteri-ous men. Strange men. Men from faraway lands like Tibet and Persia.

"Meanwhile, revolutionaries trying to overthrow the empire had taken refuge in the Shaolin Temple. Living as monks and training in Shaolin-style martial arts, they continued to plan revolt. They were dedicated, expert fighters, and the Emperor was determined to destroy them.

"He sent Bai Mei and the royal troops to Shaolin. The tem-ple was burned and almost everyone was killed, including the abbot, who died in a duel with Bai Mei.

"Two of those who escaped, a Crane master and a Monkey master, trained for ten years and then sought out Bai Mei. They were bent on vengeance. During their training, they had learned that Bai Mei's invulnerability had to have one weak point, a 'gate' that would permit entry to his human armor. But the 'gate' location varied from practitioner to practitioner, and in the ensuing fight, they couldn't find it.

"They attacked him together. They kicked his groin, but Bai Mei had succeeded in drawing his vital organs into his body. They struck his eyes; his eyelids were like steel. All the while, Bai Mei dealt one deadly counterblow after another. The two Shaolin masters were severely injured and bleeding.

"In one last desperate attempt, the Monkey master boosted the Crane fighter into a high jump and the Crane master delivered a crushing blow to the crown of Bai Mei's head. That was the point. Bai Mei's armor was lost, and it became a matched struggle among the three men.

"Bai Mei was still strong enough to fight them off and escape, but he died several days later. The two monks were also critically injured. Bai Mei had ruined their bodies, and they lay bedridden for ten years before dying."

Saihung listened intently until the conclusion of the story. Laughing with delight, he told his grandfather, "I want to be a martial hero too!"

Guan Jiuyin looked patiently at him.

"There is more to life than that, Saihung. You musn't simply decide to become a fighter or soldier. The true hero starts as a cultivated person. You must learn the 'Way.'

"Fame and fortune are predestined. Of what use is a guileful heart? Rather, constantly seek the truth, maintain your discipline, and preserve your dignity.

"Cultivate the 'Way.' Don't swim against the current. Only by swimming with it can you avoid disaster. For the bitter truth of life is this: each person is at the mercy of the tide. Sometimes one wants to go east, but one is swept to the west. Sometimes one wants to go north, but one is carried to the south. There is no choice. Finding this truth is the *Way*. The *Way* is 'Tao.'

"Tao is the flow of the universe. Tao is the Mysterious. Tao is balance. But balance can be lost; the fragile equilibrium can be destroyed by evil. Evil must sometimes be met head on. Evil must be destroyed, and those allied with Tao must then fight. If you learn to live with Tao and someday use your skills to fight evil, then perhaps you can be called a hero."

Guan Jiuyin patted Saihung fondly and stood up. Saihung remained silent. When a Chinese child was given a lesson, he was expected to contemplate it and cherish the gift until understanding came, sometimes long afterward. Saihung trusted his grandparents and the wisdom of their ways. Their world was close to the pulse of nature, a seamless blending of past and present, a mixture of memory, mythology, experience, and tradition. It was a perfect world to him—a world of giants.

Guan Jiuyin picked up a bamboo flute and walked to the doorway. Ma Sixing's last note faded away into the darkness. She soundlessly left the gazebo; her gown of autumn colors was absorbed by the darkness like winter swallowing fall. Guan Jiuyin walked to the pool's edge, his silver-haired figure was like a snow-laden tree.

He raised the flute to his lips and his song rose in the air like a pellmell flight of swallows. Gradually, his tempo fluttered down, his notes descended into a lower register, hovering over the water in an almost inaudible vibration. The pond before him had been a mirror of the dark heavens, but now its perfect surface was broken in a trembling response. Ripples went steadily to the far banks in overlapping circles as fish came swimming to Guan Jiuyin. Soon they were dancing before him, lifting their heads from the water. There were flashes of silver, orange, white, and black as the carp moved to every note in an hypnotic dance.

FIVE

Journey with Two Acolytes

EARLY THE NEXT MORNING, Guan Jiuyin summoned Saihung to the library. A servant ushered him into the large room, whispering that his grandfather would be there in a moment. Saihung walked into the quiet of the room almost reverently; he had seldom been in it.

The library contained some of Guan Jiuyin's most treasured possessions. Superbly crafted bookcases, each one a different shape from the next, lined the walls. Some were simply rectangular, with staggered shelves, while others had been made so that the contours and arrangement of the shelves formed a gigantic ideograph. The eccentric rosewood shelves contained unusual objects: precious books and scrolls, celadon bowls, Tang Dynasty horses, and jade sculptures that had taken decades to carve.

Throughout the room, more spectacular objects rested on individual polished redwood burl stands. Among them were porcelain figurines of gods and saints, and several hand-painted vases, over five feet in height. Paintings of famous mountains, portraits, and scrolls with exquisite calligraphy were hung on the walls, part of a vast collection changed seasonally. Saihung particularly admired one painting of strange and grotesque mountains.

Every object in the room represented the achievement of a master, immortal through his craft. Many of the works were centuries old, carefully preserved by connoisseurs of the esoteric and now collected by Guan Jiuyin. All together, the volumes of ancient knowledge, the jades, the porcelains, and the paintings dominated the room with their eternal beauty and seemed to insulate it from the coarse and vulgar world.

There was the whisper of a door opening and Guan Jiuyin came in. He sat down at his desk of ornately carved rosewood, inlaid mother-of-pearl, and pink Italian marble, and motioned to his servants. Two young men were escorted into the library.

The two were dressed like the Taoist acolytes Saihung had seen during the Taishan Festival. They wore long-sleeved gray robes over black pants and white leggings, and their straw sandals, well made but cut by the rocky roads, were a startling contrast to the rich carpet beneath their feet. Their faces were clear and serene beneath black coarsely woven hats and neat topknots.

Guan Jiuyin introduced each of them. The first was severe in expression, and lean-muscled. His name was Mist Through a Grove. His fellow acolyte was larger, more densely muscled, but had a ready smile. Guan Jiuyin introduced him as Sound of Clear Water. Saihung greeted each one with a formal bow.

"I am sending you away for a while with these two young men," Guan Jiuyin said to Saihung. "You're going to meet your maternal grandfather. He will oversee your education for a while. You will meet new people and learn new skills."

Saihung was overjoyed. To him it meant two new playmates, more adventure, no tutoring, and no scoldings.

The next day, the three of them left the Guan family mansion. They walked, since horses were a rare luxury, and the two acolytes, amiable and lenient, treated him with great care. Typical for him, Saihung tried to extract as much playing and candy eating as possible, and Saihung found the journey great fun. Not only could he see the inhabitants and vast farmlands of Shaanxi Province, but he got piggy-back rides as well.

Two eighteen-year-old acolytes and a nine-year-old boy together on the roads were an unusual sight, especially with Saihung carrying his bundle and a rattan rattle. But no one stopped to bother them. The acolytes' robes, topknots, and staffs were plain symbols of their position, and people respected them, still remembering the imperial days when interference with a Taoist was a capital offense. The two advanced fearlessly as they passed the many strangers, soldiers, and travelers on the roads.

During their journey, Saihung soon identified the essential

qualities of each acolyte. Mist Through a Grove was reserved, quiet, and serious. He had an abstract quality and the distant air of one who knows a great secret. A superb musician, master of most of the Chinese instruments, he carried a flute with him that he played at each day's resting place. Even-tempered and humble, he was courteous to all whom they met.

Sound of Clear Water was a skilled carpenter and had a craftsman's pragmatic outlook. Where his counterpart was more cerebral, he was fiercely and physically aggressive, earthy, and energetic. Both acolytes were renunciates and un-interested in society, but where Mist Through a Grove held himself aloof, Sound of Clear Water was vocally intolerant when other travelers occasionally or inadvertently hindered their way. When a particularly obnoxious fellow slowed the boarding of a ferry by arguing over the fare, blocking would-be passengers who had to wait under a burning sun, Sound of Clear Water shouted for him to move aside. The man glared at them. Sound of Clear Water argued violently with him and forced him aside.

Mist Through a Grove remained silent during these out-bursts. Although his temperament was different, he recognized that his brother's aggressiveness was also Taoism. The two were paired, inseparable, sworn to stand by each other, and Mist Through a Grove implicitly agreed with Sound of Clear Water's view. Perfection was all that was worth achieving, and those seeking it found the insensitive and lazy offensive.

They stayed during the nights in country inns, and all three shared the large sleeping platforms. Nights were getting colder. Saihung slept between the two acolytes, beneath layers of cotton quilting on clay platforms with wood-burning chambers. The acolytes placed him thus to comfort him, so far away from home. Saihung took advantage of the situation, snuggling up to one and then the other. But one night, Mist Through a Grove noticed Saihung sitting up, looking into the room.

Mist Through a Grove

"What's wrong, Saihung?"

Saihung said nothing. He was uncertain about explaining his fear. But the shadows that silhouetted on the thin paper windows, the strange scratching sound against the wall, indicated a demon or possibly an ogre. His fear quickly escalated. After all, the two acolytes were still young. Perhaps a demon was coming to eat them all!

"Is that—is that a demon?" Saihung asked in a terrified whisper.

"Where?" asked Mist Through a Grove.

Saihung pointed nervously.

Sound of Clear Water also sat up.

"Hey! How can anyone sleep with you two whispering?" He looked in the direction of Saihung's finger and jumped.

"Oh no! A demon!" cried Sound of Clear Water.

Saihung hid behind both of them.

"Good thing *Da Shi* gave us a talisman to ward off evil," shrieked Sound of Clear Water. "But it only works for two!"

Terrified, Saihung clutched his tiger-tooth talisman.

"Can you see it?" he asked.

"Of course I can!" boomed back Sound of Clear Water. "Can't you? There! He's coming through the window. He's got red hair, green skin, big warts, sharp teeth, and he's drooling. He's got a big burlap bag."

"A bag?"

"Yes, you know, the kind they put little boys in? Now, Brother and I here are too tough and sinewy. I think he wants a plump little rich kid."

Saihung screamed.

Mist Through a Grove stood up and pulled Saihung out of bed. Saihung resisted frantically as the acolyte dragged him to the shadow.

"Do you see a demon?" he asked softly.

"No," Saihung conceded. "But Brother can!"

"Let me tell you something, Saihung. Only the dying or very ill see demons. You aren't either one." He pushed the

Sound of Clear Water

window open. "Look outside. Don't you see that these tree branches make moving shadows and scrape against the wall?"

Saihung looked up at him. "You mean there are no demons?"

Mist Through a Grove smiled reassuringly. Saihung had found the truth himself.

Saihung ran back to the sleeping platform, where Sound of Clear Water was laughing, and jumped furiously on top of him. "You lied! You lied!" he shouted as he ineffectually hit the acolyte. Sound of Clear Water only laughed all the more as he lay back and let Saihung kick and punch him.

The tenth morning of their journey was cloudy and overcast. Autumn had deepened into intense cold. The trees bordering Shaanxi's grain fields were a dazzling display of reds, oranges, and yellows—as if their branches were fragments of a crystallized and shattered spectrum. Saihung pulled his jacket tightly against the stiff wind and took a look into the distance. On the horizon was the misty profile of the Huashan mountain range.

The mountains rose with a towering suddenness that accentuated the flatness of the surrounding lowlands. They were lofty, proud, rugged mountains, with cliffs so close to perpendicular that few people ventured up their heights. Huashan was magnificent and invincible in its inaccessibility; its unearthly grandeur was the perfect Taoist setting.

But Saihung's childish impression of Huashan was that of a giant's forbidding citadel. He was frightened and begged to go home.

"Brothers, this isn't fun anymore," he said when they stopped for a rest. "Let's go back now and find another game to play."

The acolytes looked at each other. Sound of Clear Water went to Saihung's bag and took out Saihung's rattle.

"Here, Little Brother, why not have some fun and see what's up there?" he said.

"I want to go home," said Saihung, turning his back to the acolyte.

"How about candy apples?" asked Mist Through a Grove. "They say the best ones are made on the mountain."

"No. No, it's no fun anymore."

The two acolytes looked in exasperation at the balking boy. Sound of Clear Water sighed in frustration.

"Ah, Saihung," said Mist Through a Grove. "Didn't we tell you the secret?"

The acolyte laid a friendly hand on Saihung's shoulder. He was shrewd; Saihung's curiosity was immediately piqued.

"What secret?"

Sound of Clear Water understood instantly.

"Shh! Don't tell him! We promised *Da Shi!*"

"Tell me! Tell me!"

"No! Don't tell him!"

Mist Through a Grove hushed his brother. "No," he said seriously, "We should tell him."

"Yes! Yes! Tell me!"

"Saihung, we wanted it to be a surprise. Now we'll have to tell you: not only your maternal grandfather but your grandfather, Guan Jiuyin, are waiting for you up there."

"Really?"

"Yes. Now come, we have to reach an inn by tonight. To-morrow we begin climbing the mountain. Even that will take two days."

"All right," said Saihung, cheerful again. He turned to Sound of Clear Water. "Brother, will you give me a ride?"

"Me?" returned Sound of Clear Water. "Certainly not. You're nearly sixty pounds. My back's almost broken from all the other times."

"I don't like you anymore!" Saihung pouted. "I'll ask Older Brother."

"Don't look now, but Older Brother is down the road already," laughed Sound of Clear Water.

Saihung sat down obstinately. "I'm not walking."

"Suit yourself," shrugged the acolyte as he took up his bag and staff and walked away.

"I'm not moving!" screamed Saihung.

Sound of Clear Water quickly caught up with his brother. The two had barely gone a hundred paces when the trio was complete again.

SIX

Entering Another World

THEY REACHED the foot of Hua-
shan the next day. Sheer cliff walls soared into the sky and
vertical faces of granite seemed to offer no opening for travelers. There was only a single trail that led into the mountains.

It was a stiff, four-hour climb through two mountain passes
and down a long valley to reach the Qingkeping Terrace, a
beautiful pine forest where several mountain streams con-
verged. Here was a small temple where they stayed the night
to refresh themselves. Other Taoist priests and acolytes were
also guests, and the two acolytes chatted amiably with them.

The setting of the temple was breathtaking in its beauty.
The rest of Huashan stood like heavenly ramparts beyond sil-
houettes of gnarled and ancient pines. The sound of waterfalls
was a constant calming music, and the cool, pure air was invig-
orating. Nature reigned supreme here; no human violation
was evident. The mountains stood in their original purity.

The next day the three travelers started on their climb of the
first of Huashan's five main peaks, the North Peak. This high
spire of granite served as the sentry peak, with the other four
set far behind. It was the only access to the whole of Huashan,
and the climb was arduous. Two stones with carved calligraphy alluded to the danger of the climb with the words
"Change Your Mind" and "Safety Is to Turn Back." The acolytes led Saihung past that point to another rock called the
Recollection Stone, where the advice changed to "Think of
One's Parents" and "Advance Forward Courageously."

They scaled the North Peak in three main sections by way of
a narrow path only two feet wide. Long segments of the trail
were actually stairs and rock ladders cut into the cliffside, with
iron chains provided for assistance. Climbing the steps of the

Qingkeping Terrace. Note the caves high in the cliffs,

青柯坪

坪柯青

北斗坪

where monks sequestered themselves in meditation

Thousand-Foot Precipice, traversing the Hundred-Foot Gorge, and finally inching up the Heaven's Furrow took many grueling hours before the three reached the summit.

The North Peak was a blade of rock thrust straight up from the mountains below. Its clean sides presented only narrow crevices where shrubs and pines rooted sparsely. A rising spine with an apex barely wide enough to stand on, there was no plateau at its summit, only a path of eroded steps leading through two stone gates to a small temple built astride the knife-edge ridge.

Foundations extended down each side into the slope. The temple was barely twenty feet in width. Its façade was made of brick and stucco with a sloped terra-cotta roof supported by two plain red pillars. The temple, accommodating to its uneven foundation, was composed of a succession of tiny buildings, perched in a straight line like saddles on the mountain.

The three walked in single file to the temple. Turning his head from side to side was enough for Saihung to see both sides of the mountain plunge swiftly away. As they came to the front portico of the temple, Saihung saw the foundations of uneven hand-made bricks and was not at all assured of the building's stability.

A cool breeze caressed them as they paused at the doorway. The sun was just beginning to set. In the far distance Saihung could see the Shaanxi basin, checkered with farmland stretching to the horizon. Through distant clouds surging like the backs of stampeding animals, the silver ribbon of the Yellow River was a twisting blur. The sun became a bright red glow, and the entire panorama was lit by its warm light. Huashan turned golden. The world was far away and it seemed as if they had attained the first level of heaven itself.

The *Da Shi*—Grand Master of Huashan—met them inside the temple. All three immediately knelt down and bowed low. Saihung was reminded of having mistaken the Grand Master for a statue, but now the Grand Master seemed very much alive. The Grand Master raised them and smiled in greeting.

The Grand Master was the patriarch of all the other abbots, priests, and ascetics of Huashan. Slender and tall, he moved gracefully and lightly, while his ever-erect figure dominated the room. His arching brows were like wisps of snow, his beard like a cascade. His face was only slightly wrinkled around his brow, and his eyes were always serene and half-lidded as if concealing an inner light. A scar cut across the right side of his mouth, suggesting his fighting past. The Grand Master looked ancient, yet his energetic aura was readily apparent. He embodied the same character as the mountain. He seemed as if he had been there from primordial time.

The two acolytes shut the heavy temple doors. In the darkness of the temple interior, with three strange men, on a faraway mountaintop, Saihung grew apprehensive. He looked at the two acolytes, but they remained silent. He turned to the Grand Master, who was also quiet. The Grand Master had just returned from a month-long retreat of complete solitude and silence and did not talk easily. Breath was life's force not to be wasted. Instead, he sat watchfully.

"Where is Grandfather?" Saihung demanded.

"He's not here," said Sound of Clear Water.

"You tricked me again!" Saihung shouted. "I'll never forgive you!" As he burst out loudly, he was inwardly surprised. The two acolytes had laughed at his tantrums before, but they now stood with serious expressions.

"Take me home! Take me home!" Saihung exploded. In a fury, he kicked over a chair, chipping it. Sound of Clear Water, maker of the temple furniture, looked visibly pained. Saihung noticed this and continued to knock over as much as possible. The acolytes rushed crazily around, saving furniture and porcelain from his rampage. Saihung was screaming, crying, and hitting them all the while.

The Grand Master calmly left the room, leaving the two acolytes to cope with him.

Saihung's tantrum lasted over an hour until he had cried himself hoarse. He whimpered in a corner, completely spent.

The journey, the climb, the high altitude, and his own outburst had worn him out.

He lay crumpled like a whipped animal, too weary to fight any longer. The Grand Master returned and stood over him. Reaching out, he touched his right index finger to Saihung's forehead and Saihung's mind went blank.

The Grand Master spoke for the first time.

"You are in another world now. From this day on, your life will change completely. You shall become a vehicle to receive. You have entered Taoism."

PART TWO

EARLY YEARS ON HUASHAN

SEVEN

The Grand Mountains

Huashan—the Grand Mountains—was an isolated religious and educational community. In mountains that were themselves objects of worship and legend, the Taoists researched and preserved special knowledge, educated coming generations, and pursued reclusive lives of mysticism and meditation.

Among the five major peaks were located individual temples and enclaves with their own masters, abbots, priests, and practitioners. Although they all placed themselves under the leadership of the Grand Master, each was autonomous. Considerable variation existed over the aspect of Taoism each emphasized: some stressed the scriptures, sorcery, or martial arts, and some, like the sect Saihung entered, stressed hygiene, internal alchemy, and asceticism. But there were still certain basic principles shared by all the Taoists, and there was much dialogue and interchange.

This rich diversity made Huashan an ideal educational institution. At a time and place where education was the privilege of a few, it functioned like a university, and boys from the age of nine were accepted as students. Some were candidates for the priesthood, but the majority were sent for a conventional parochial education. The hundreds of boys living in the temples learned all the academic subjects from scholar priests expert in their fields.

The number of students entering Taoism as monks was considerably smaller. In order to pursue some aspect of Taoism as a specialty, one had to serve and study with a master who functioned as a spiritual father. He not only passed on his own knowledge, but carefully sent his disciples to learn from other masters as well. A master naturally limited himself to only a

The northern view of Huashan, showing the foothills

and the northern, eastern, and western peaks

few disciples; through them would be transmitted the full Taoist tradition.

Aside from teaching, most advanced practitioners on Huashan pursued their own research and practices. Taoism was limitless, a lifelong pursuit of higher and higher knowledge. Some Taoists devoted themselves to herbalism, medicine, poetry, calligraphy, or music. Others were spiritual mediums, oracles, diviners. Still others pursued internal alchemy in the quest for immortality. And there were also men on Huashan who were solely hermits and recluses. Genuine renunciates, some of whom were already considered immortal, they rarely associated with anyone.

Huashan's temples were all united under the philosophy of renunciation and asceticism. Other sects of Taoism were known for other specialties; the single-minded pursuit of spiritual knowledge and self-perfection characterized Huashan.

The task of initiating Saihung into this rich Taoist tradition, and changing him from a spoiled and mischievous child to a complete and spiritual man, did not promise to be easy. But the Grand Master was wise. The very reason that Saihung would be difficult was also the reason for Saihung's training to begin now: he was only a boy. A boy had to be given the chance to grow freely but he also had to be cultivated. The tree that was to grow tall had to be nurtured from a seedling. The Grand Master directed the acolytes to raise Saihung gently.

The Grand Master knew that Saihung would gradually accept life on the mountain because the mountain, so pure and natural, so imbued with the aura of Taoists who had reached their realization there, would influence him strongly. Little needed to be forced. Saihung would absorb naturally. The first full day after Saihung's arrival on Huashan was already the beginning of his education, as the acolytes took him climbing on the peaks.

The North Peak's ridge trail, the Imperial Way, was the way to the other four peaks. It was simply a narrow ledge cut into a nearly perpendicular cliff. In some places, overhanging rock made it all the more difficult to pass. The drop, veiled as it was by mist, was still dizzying to contemplate, and Saihung clung tightly to Sound of Clear Water's hand.

The twisted, swaybacked ridge dipped down steeply to the foot of the Middle Peak. Saihung passed groves of dense pines with tiny temples hidden within them. At the foot of the Middle Peak, they began another ascent on the Dragon Ridge.

That straight, acutely angled ridge had steps cut up its spine. Although it made a hard climb, the Taoists had established the trail in this difficult way because it followed their concepts of geomancy. Trails that followed the lines of the mountain, rather than violating it by switchback trails, placed the climber in harmony with the mountain. The Dragon Ridge Trail faithfully followed the ridge line to the summit, but mystic harmony or not, it was dangerous; the steps were eroded and there were no railings.

It was a two-hour hike from the North Peak to the spot where the Dragon Ridge reached the Gold Lock Pass. During that time they passed both masters and disciples. Some greeted them, others strolled in contemplation, and some were busy carrying provisions to their temples. At the Gold Lock Pass, the trail connected with a circular one that led in a clockwise direction to the Middle, East, South, and West peaks and then back to the Pass.

They went from the Middle Peak, with its single massive temple and pine forests, to the East Peak. This high point was also known as the Morning Sun Cliff, because the sunrises seen from its summit were legendary. Saihung would frequently see future dawning days there.

The East Peak Monastery was plain stucco and tile and was composed of groups of four-square buildings set in quadrangles. There were also smaller huts of wood and clay. As they passed a hut set behind an iron bell topped with a stone cup that collected dew, Saihung saw a willow-thin man sunning himself on the terrace. He wore gray robes and a black hat with a jade rectangle sewn to its front. The acolytes told Sai-

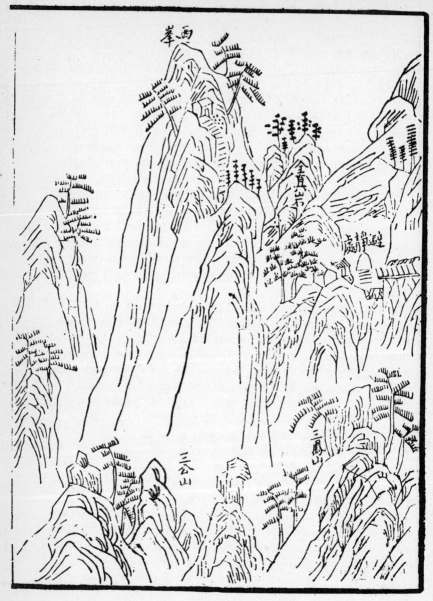

The southern view of Huashan, including (from left to right)

the West Peak, South Peak, Cliff Path, and East Peak

hung that he was a sorcerer. There were other men in front of individual shrines who sat silently and seemed as powerful. Even the acolytes did not know them all, but said that they must all be of the same stature to be on the East Peak.

Further down the trail they stopped at a high place that overlooked a terrace on an outcropping peak, the Chessboard Pavilion. So high and isolated was that peak that only chasms formed the background behind it. In the tenth century, the first Emperor of the Song Dynasty wanted Huashan for its military strategic value. But the Taoists wanted to keep Huashan sacred. Chen Tuan the Immortal challenged the Emperor to a game of chess, the winner of the game to take Huashan. On that isolated pinnacle the Emperor lost game after game. Finally, Chen Tuan even predicted the Emperor's every move, and the Emperor finally conceded. The Chessboard Pavilion was thus named; Huashan remained Taoist.

The trio came to a precipice and there they faced the most treacherous portion of the trail, the Cliff Path. The path was over a series of wooden planks set atop iron supports drilled into the sheer cliff. There was not even a railing to bar a straight fall of over 3,000 feet—only iron chains pegged to the cliff on which to clutch. Sound of Clear Water strapped Saihung to his back, and they ventured out. The boards flexed and creaked. The wind rushing along the rock face blew Saihung's sweat cold. He closed his eyes tightly. He was completely suspended in midair, and he clung in fright to the acolyte.

The South Peak was the highest peak of Huashan, a massive piece of rock with sides so sheer that no trees could grow on them and even heavy snow found very few resting places. China stretched away in all directions from this crowning point, and the Huang, Luo, and Wei rivers were slender strands on the edge of the sky. The peak boasted a spring-fed granite basin that remained unfrozen even in winter. The acolytes also showed Saihung the South Peak Temple, where he would live.

The final peak was the West Peak. A rugged path led up the ridge to a monastery perched impossibly on the side of the mountain. This again was geomancy. The Taoists revered the "dragon's pulse," the meridians of the earth. These energy pathways had certain "power spots," like the acupuncture points of the human body. The Taoists built their temples and shrines over those spots, even though the locations, such as on the North and West Peaks, frequently coincided with the very crest. The buildings were always of natural materials, primarily brick, stone, and wood, devoid of ornamentation, and were in such harmony with the surrounding terrain that they were invisible even from a short distance. The West Peak temple was a typical example. Its halls were set on a sixty-degree slope and were hidden by rocks and trees.

The West Peak, curiously cleft, also had its share of legends, and the most romantic gave it its alternate name, the Lotus Lamp Peak. The legend recounted the love affair between one of the Jade Emperor's seven daughters and a handsome cowherd. Goddess and mortal lived together until she was missed by her father. When the Jade Emperor found that she had not only given herself to a cowherd but had also borne him a child, he imprisoned her beneath the West Peak. Her son, Chen Xiang, grew up and found a Taoist sorcerer to teach him. When his pupil was ready, the Taoist gave Chen Xiang a divine axe, which he used to fight off the demon guard and cleave the West Peak. But the reunion was interrupted by the guard's return with all of heaven's armies. The son fought with the axe, and the mother used magic and a lotus lamp as a weapon to repulse the soldiers. The Jade Emperor, touched by Chen Xiang's devotion, forgave them, and the West Peak with its cleft was known thereafter as the Lotus Lamp Peak.

Views and stories were Saihung's first impression of Huashan. He saw it as a mountain of precipitous height. A place where vistas were alternately obscured by clouds or revealed in distant peaks and valleys. A place of legend and mythology, unusual and powerful inhabitants, and tiny temples nestled

South Peak

on narrow ledges. Huashan was the mysterious and the sacred. Even Saihung, indignant as he was for being forced to live there, was awestruck by its beauty, fascinated by the strange men, and affected by the pervading air of reverence.

The acolytes took Saihung to the Grand Master's temple, the South Peak Shrine of the Jade Fertility Well, a large compound of buildings and courtyards enclosed within a brick and stucco wall. The architecture was at once traditionally Chinese and yet somewhat asymmetrical in its ground plan. The acolytes explained to Saihung that the rooms and buildings had been arranged to echo the patterns of the constellations.

The main hall of the temple was the Grand Master's own residence. Before it was a large bronze incense burner, symbol of Huashan. A flight of steps led to the main entrance. Two bronze cranes stood at the base of the stone steps, two lanterns at the head. The columns and lintels that supported the temple were of carved wood, and plaques with calligraphy adorned the entrance. The two plaques that flanked the main doors urged, "Leave All Worldly Thoughts" and "Only Vegetarians May Enter."

The temple, like all those on Huashan, had a plain appearance. The stone was eroded, and the wood was weathered. But the halls of material poverty were rich in spiritual feeling. Fragrant streams of incense flowed throughout the corridors, the sounds of chanting could always be heard softly from unseen rooms, and windows framed lofty views of faraway mountains.

The temple was maintained by the monks themselves. Every menial task from cleaning and cooking to repairing the buildings was shared equally among them. Rank exempted no one save the Grand Master, and the practical upkeep of the temple also encouraged cooperation between all the monks.

In the following months, the two acolytes helped Saihung adjust to temple life. They slept on the same platform, and their mornings began even before the sun came up. Monastic life was a daily succession of religious and maintenance duties

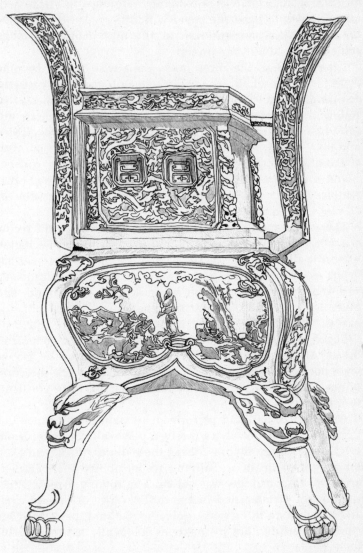

Bronze incense urn in the courtyard of the South Peak Temple

that began immediately on waking. Saihung's first task each morning was to open the paper windows so that the sunlight would dry the condensation in the high mountain room, which was cold all year around.

After washing, the three made their way in the dawning light to the main hall, where all the temple members gathered to pray and recite Taoist sutras before breakfast. The meals that followed were vegetarian and extremely frugal. Breakfast was only one bowl of rice porridge, a dish of pickled vegetables, and tea.

Saihung's mornings were devoted to receiving a conventional education, either from the acolytes or in classes at other temples. Beside reading, writing, history, and other subjects, he also learned acrobatics and calisthenics.

There was another sutra recital before lunch. Sutra recital was both for devotion and for training the breath. Recitation was in itself a type of *qigong*, and all the monks were serious about recitation—except Saihung. He found it difficult to keep still and during each session he smiled, looked around, and mumbled cheerfully but uncomprehendingly along with the others.

Lunch consisted of noodles and vegetables and sometimes bread. All the meals were taken in utter silence; the monks were not even permitted to look at one another. The direction of one's concentration, even during meals, was to be constantly inward.

After lunch, Saihung performed his own maintenance duties while the two acolytes received personal instruction from the Grand Master. By prescribing these duties, the Grand Master sought to instill in Saihung responsibility and perseverance. But responsibility was not quick in coming. Irrepressible, thoroughly disinterested in the dull severity of monasticism, and much more interested in playing, Saihung performed his chores cheerfully, but his methods frequently led to unfortunate results.

Windows of delicate latticework and paper were kicked open gleefully. Sweeping was done with exaggerated swinging. Flowers were watered by the bucketful—from upper balconies. Even the sutra books were transformed by his imagination. Airing out the accordion-folded sutras to prevent mildew gave Saihung the chance to hold one end and then fling the other across the courtyard; dozens of feet of holy scripture flew through the air to land haphazardly.

Retribution was always swift whenever Saihung became mischievous in his chores. Sometimes he was denied dinner. At other times, such as after his rough treatment of the scriptures, Sound of Clear Water spanked him. The acolyte was immune to Saihung's crocodile tears and dispensed justice dispassionately.

Saihung was given more difficult tasks when he became settled. Cultivating greenhouse vegetables, raising chickens and fish (to be eaten on feast days by guests, or by monks who were ill), and gathering wood were the more complex assignments. In these cases, he was given no instruction and had to talk to other masters in order to solve any problems. It was the Grand Master's way of instilling initiative and a sense of the necessity of learning.

In the later afternoons, Saihung accompanied the two acolytes on walks around the mountains. During these hours they taught him further, explained things about Huashan and nature, or just relaxed.

After evening recitation, and a dinner of vegetables, noodles, and steamed bread, there was time for more study, calisthenics, or personal affairs. It was time for bed around ten o'clock.

This schedule was carried on seven days a week, and Saihung slowly accepted Taoist monastic life. He even did his best to carry out his own self-created mission by cheering up the severe temple atmosphere with jokes, pranks, and affectionate songs. Many of the temple members did seem to enjoy the child's bright presence. In spite of his rebellious naughtiness, they liked Saihung's cheerful and unrestrained personality. Taoism was preparing to raise another disciple, but the disciple in exchange brought a little laughter to its hallowed halls.

EIGHT

Learning from the Natural World

NATURE ITSELF PROVIDED many learning opportunities for Saihung, and the two acolytes took these occasions not only to explain the world to him but also to convey basic Taoist concepts. Saihung had great curiosity. In the temple and in walks around the mountains, he saw many things that aroused his inquisitiveness. The explanations the acolytes gave were designed both to satisfy his interest and to prepare him for asceticism.

As the three awoke one morning to the sonorous tones of the temple bell, Mist Through a Grove pointed to a cat who often slept with them. The temple had many cats to catch mice, and this brown and white one had adopted the three of them.

"The Taoists are great naturalists, Saihung. They study the animals in order to understand how they stay healthy and how they remain with the divine. All that we on the mountain do is simple and natural and no more out of the ordinary than what animals do. But what common people and Taoists perceive to be the activity of animals are often two different things."

The cat was asleep on the edge of the blue quilt, her tail and nose tucked under her folded paws. Mist Through a Grove continued his explanation:

"The early Taoists wanted to remain healthy and retard the aging process. They believed that people aged because their internal energy leaked out. In order to find a way to retain it in the body, they found inspiration in animals like our cat here. They concluded that one way an animal sealed its energy in was by sleeping curled up, effectively closing off its anus and other passages where the energy might escape. This is how our cat sleeps.

"Now look at her abdomen, rising and falling so gently. The cat's breathing is natural and easy. The Taoists also found and confirmed that unhindered breathing filling the entire abdomen was beneficial."

The cat awoke when Mist Through a Grove nudged it. She opened her eyes and pricked up her ears attentively. Mist Through a Grove continued his lesson.

"She wakes instantly, not like humans who are lazy, drowsy, and stiff. See how she stretches. Even the cat knows calisthenics and uses them to maintain her system. The Taoists know that exercise is essential to good health.

"What if our cat gets sick? After all, she eats mice and rats, both very dirty animals. She supplements her diet with herbs and grass in order to clean her system.

"Finally, the cat is spiritual. She meditates. When she sits at the window sill or in front of a mouse hole, she is unmoving and concentrates just like our masters. You've seen her waiting for a rat. Nothing distracts her. Her mind is only on one point. She can sit for almost an entire day at one hole until the rat comes out and she catches it. Yin and yang. Perfect stillness and concentration, perfect action and strength.

"Our cat does not need teachers. The cat teaches itself. It preserves energy, knows the art of breathing, heals itself, and is skilled in meditative concentration. Study the cat, Saihung. Everything you need to learn, she knows already."

That afternoon, the two acolytes took Saihung to a densely forested section of Huashan. They walked toward a high cliff where pines clung by twisted roots to its very brink. Beneath one lushly verdant pine was a large crane that stood motionless on one leg. Although it seemed aware of their presence, it did not stir. All the animals near Huashan recognized that the Taoists never harmed any of them, and the crane stood there confidently, dominatingly.

"Early Taoists wanted to learn each animal's secret," explained Sound of Clear Water, "and practice it themselves. In the beginning, they did not understand everything. Like you looking at the cat this morning, they only suspected certain things.

"Look at that bird. How vain it is! Birds are like that. Arrogant. Posey. But look at it again, Saihung. It's so big! How can it fly? How can it stand on one thin leg like that?

"It can only be *qi* that is responsible. Breath mixed with the bird's energy lightens its body enough to fly. Filling itself up with air, it can lift off or stand on one leg.

"But why is it standing on one leg? Because, like our cat, it is locking off the body to conserve its energy. The Taoists adopted certain meditation postures, and perfected their theory of longevity, from looking at the crane's three distinct locks. Its head is tilted back in the head lock and its eyes stare up at the psychic center in its forehead, its chest is made full, to lock its diaphragm, and one leg is tucked in to close the anus.

"You can see other animals using the body locks to conserve their energy. The dog sleeps curled up. The deer puts one hoof against its anus while sleeping. Observe, Saihung. All nature knows the secrets of longevity except foolish humanity."

As Saihung grew older, Sound of Clear Water would carry him no longer, and he had to climb Huashan's steep paths on his own. It was difficult, and he grew tired easily. The two acolytes used the deer and the tiger as lessons to help him further.

"Whether you are moving uphill or down, you find the way tiring, don't you?" asked Mist Through a Grove.

"You don't know how to move," said Sound of Clear Water.

"You've seen many deer," continued Mist Through a Grove. "When they run uphill, they almost seem to float up and their hooves seem to barely touch down, because the deer know how to make their internal energy move upward.

"When a deer is running, all the energy is in its extremities—at the hooves, tail, and antlers. The deer is powerful. Through its use of body locks, it maintains its internal energy and circulates it outward. The outside signs of this are its tail and antlers, both imbued with such great life force that as a tonic, they can revitalize the most elderly of men. Since the deer sends all its energy upward, it can easily run uphill.

"You will be able to learn methods of circulating your internal energy later. But for now, if you have to go uphill, think of the deer. Learn from them how to move effortlessly."

"There's a special way to move downhill, too," said Sound of Clear Water. "What's the worst thing about walking downhill? Isn't it that jarring feeling on your bones? The Taoists noticed this and looked to the tiger for inspiration. Nothing moves downhill like a tiger. He is unhurried, relaxed, loose. He slinks down the hill. His every step falls effortlessly into place. He is lithe and sleek, not like a person who stumbles and descends clumsily.

"The tiger is the symbol of strength in the bones and sinews. Coming down the hill, he uses relaxed strength and flexible joints and just eases down. He never jars his bones, because he is resilient. In all the animal kingdom, the tiger has some of the strongest bones—so strong that they too can be used as tonic medicine.

"So when descending, use the relaxed strength of the tiger to slow yourself, and keep the joints loose to protect your bones. When ascending, make your body light, using the rising energy of the deer to make your climb effortless."

There were lakes and streams in the mountains around Huashan, and the acolytes had taken Saihung on a short herb-gathering expedition when they stopped beside a lake for lunch. It was late spring, the lake was alive with dragonflies, birds, butterflies, frogs, and tortoises.

Saihung splashed water at the two acolytes, and they responded playfully by almost pushing him into the lake. Saihung, struggling to get away from their tickling, fell into the mud. There was much laughter as he glumly rinsed off his clothes and sat on a sunny rock waiting for them to dry.

As he waited, he broke off a long reed and poked at an old

tortoise. The tortoise withdrew its head. Saihung tapped each foot until they too were withdrawn, and finally even the tail was inside. The tortoise waited for Saihung's attention to flag and then lumbered off to another rock. Saihung watched its steady gait.

"Look at that old fellow," whispered Sound of Clear Water. "Trying to be so dignified after a kid has poked him. But do you know what, Saihung? That tortoise will probably outlive you. The tortoise has great longevity because it never rushes. Our masters always walk leisurely because they know that rushing shortens one's life."

"How about the abbot of the North Peak Temple?" broke in Saihung irreverently. "His round head's so old and wrinkled that he looks like a turtle already!"

The two acolytes laughed.

"Yes, he does, doesn't he?" giggled Sound of Clear Water. "Let's nickname him Master Turtle."

After some more uproarious speculation about whether Master Turtle could rush even if his temple caught fire, Sound of Clear Water continued his lesson.

"Look at that other tortoise sunning himself. His head stretches way out, and he looks upward at his third eye. He's meditating. All his energy travels upward. And look at that old one sleeping. Everything's inside his shell. What's more obvious? He's practicing the three locks, and all his energy remains within his shell."

Saihung studied the two tortoises.

"But I don't want to be humpbacked like a tortoise," he complained. "And definitely not fat and ugly like those frogs over there!"

"Fat!" exclaimed Mist Through a Grove. "O-ho! Those frogs aren't fat and ugly. In fact, they are creatures very much adored by Taoists!"

"Ugh!" said Saihung.

The two acolytes sat down beside Saihung. The afternoon was hot and clear. Taking off their sandals and leggings, they dangled their feet in the cool, limpid water. Mist Through a Grove pointed to one enormous bullfrog with glistening green skin and a fine pattern of black spots like a spray of flung oil. The frog squatted in a massive lump, and its contrasting white throat inflated to an impossible bulge.

"The frog," explained Mist Through a Grove, "is a master of *qigong*. He is constantly exercising the three locks. Squatting locks the anus. Inflating his chest locks the diaphragm, and his eyes look constantly at his third eye, locking his head. With its mind on the divine and its body locked in its meditation posture, it practices *qigong* and permits no *qi* to escape. The frog's *qigong* is the best of all. He can jump unusual distances, and he can store tremendous amounts of *qi*."

Mist Through a Grove splashed through the water and, after several hilarious failures, caught a frog. He brought it back to Saihung and held it by its shoulders. The frog was pitifully thin and elongated.

"You see, Saihung," said Sound of Clear Water. "A frog isn't fat. It is its ability with *qigong* that makes it appear that way. We Taoists emulate the frog—so great at *qigong*, so stable in meditation."

Similar lessons were repeated over and over until the concepts began to take hold. Soon, the acolytes moved on to a critical lesson. Saihung would be approaching adolescence, and the acolytes introduced him to the topics of sexuality and celibacy.

Saihung had seen animals mating in the spring and had demanded to know what they were doing. The acolytes explained the cycle of reproduction fully and openly and even showed him human sexual function through books and pictures. Mating was a natural event, and the Taoists never denied anything that was natural. But the acolytes pointed out that continence was also natural. After they had fully explained mating, they gave this lesson:

"Animals mate only during spring," Mist Through a Grove

told Saihung. "In some species, male and female do not even intermingle a great deal. All the animals practice celibacy, and in so doing they preserve their life force."

"Look at the achievements of our masters," continued Sound of Clear Water. "If you want to preserve your health, attain longevity, and pierce life's mysteries, you must seal in the life force though the three locks, and practice *qigong* and meditation to retain and circulate the life force that is rooted in *jing*, or sexual essence."

They showed him more anatomical diagrams.

"The body has different centers, all in a line," said Mist Through a Grove. "Each one, from the bottom of the torso to the crown of the head, will provide certain powers to the practitioner. Energy is needed to open these centers. The highest point is the crown, and it is difficult to refine one's energy and raise it that high. In order to do this, *jing* reacts with breath and becomes *qi*. *Qi* is circulated and transformed into *spirit*. It is spirit energy that reaches the top.

"The animals, through the practices we showed you and with the use of celibacy, preserve their *jing* and remain in the spiritual. Should you engage in sex you will deplete your *jing*. No *jing* means no *qi*. No *qi* means no spirituality."

The two acolytes took him to the monastery schools and showed him boys of varying ages so that Saihung would know in advance of body changes that would happen to him. They wanted him to have an easy transition into puberty and prepared him thoroughly. On festival days, they took him to the North Peak Temple, Huashan's only public temple. There, they drove home their point about celibacy by pointing out married men.

"Look how wrinkled that one is," said Sound of Clear Water. "He's probably no older than forty but his face is wrinkled, his hair is gray and falling out. Why? No *jing*. He expends too much of it and does not have knowledge of the locks and upward circulation. He's stooped over, his breathing is shallow, and his body appears stiff and brittle. Compared to any Taoist here, he is unequal to any one of them even twice his age."

Saihung could see the differences. The Taoists did seem different from ordinary men, and he began to favor the way of the celibate ascetic even before his adolescence. He now knew only the pure Taoist world, where, free of contradicting temptations, the acolytes' teachings took hold. Saihung soon aspired to the spiritual heights achieved by the masters.

NINE

The Wisdom of Cycles

SAIHUNG WAS eleven when he and the two acolytes discussed the cycles of life. It was a stunning summer's day and the air, even at the summit of the West Peak, was warm and balmy. Saihung gazed out across the deep valley, following the cadence of mountain ridges to the horizon, and reveled in the sky's sleek blue canopy.

Mist Through a Grove gave him time to enjoy the view before he summed up all the informal nature lessons they had had until then.

"Everything is cyclical," he said. "The world follows the seasons. The seasons—spring, summer, fall, and winter—follow one another.

"The animals live in harmony with the seasons. In spring, they mate. In summer, they bear their young. In autumn, they nurture their young and prepare for winter. In winter, they either maintain stillness or migrate, but everything is aimed at survival. Rodents burrow. Turtles and bears hibernate. The weak die."

"Each year, you should also follow the seasons. Spring is the time for new growth, movement, exercise, and fresh activity. Summer is the time to release your vigor fully, to work on endeavors begun. Autumn is a time of harvest but also of preparation for winter. Winter is a time when nothing moves. Everything withdraws into the earth or dies. That is when you should withdraw into yourself and meditate.

"The course of your life will also follow the patterns of the seasons. Now you are in the spring of your life. You must go forward, bursting like the buds on the trees. You must act any way you feel. You're a child and if you didn't act mischievous or playful, you wouldn't be normal. But as you grow older, remember that the spring is also the optimum time to plant the seeds of your future.

"In the summer of your life, be a strong, proud, and able youth. Cultivate yourself, make achievements, explore, leave nothing undone that should be started. Do everything, satisfy all the emotions, but do so with moderation and within the context of your philosophy. Whether you must sometimes be active or retreating, shining or veiled, good or even evil, you must come forth and do great things in the summer of your life.

"In autumn, you will reap what you have sown. Once you're in middle age, you will have set your life's course. The consequences of your earlier acts and decisions will begin to appear. How important it is to reach this stage with no regrets! This should be the time you begin to slow down, to teach others, collect your rewards, and make preparations for old age.

"Old age is winter. You become still. Your hair becomes ice and snow. You meditate, contemplate life's meaning, and prepare for death."

Sound of Clear Water picked up the theme. Saihung was receptive, and the acolyte spoke quietly and slowly.

"Many men are afraid of death because they are ignorant of what it is and when it will come. They think death is an ending. It isn't. It is a transformation. Life does not cease. It goes in cycles like the seasons.

"No one in your family has died yet, but you've seen death. You've seen fallen trees, withered wildflowers, corpses of animals in the snows. But have they all ceased to exist? Is death to be a simple fall into immobility and decay? Whether it is a person or animal, the fact is that death is only the casting off of a shell.

"What you are, what I am, what the animals are, is something intangible, indestructible, formless—a collection of ancestral memories mixed with traces of the past cosmos. We are spirits, and each individual spirit has existed from the very beginning and will continue hurtling through space, changing and evolving, into infinity.

"What you know to be animals were not always animals and will not always remain animals. They are only taking this shell during this lifetime. They are spirits who have come into this world to learn things that are important to them as individuals, and to achieve a divine purpose. But when they come to earth they need a shield, a shell, a body. The body is not the true individual. It is only a vessel. When it is time to go on to another reality, the bodies that have been the vessels are discarded and the spirit goes on.

"You cannot wear two sets of clothing. You cannot stay in one building and simultaneously enter another. The shell that is your body must be used up. It will get worn, broken, destroyed. But the spirit is never destroyed, and there is no need to be frightened.

"Men are also afraid because they do not know when death will come. This is just one of the curses the gods have placed on humanity. As punishment for man's perversity and evil, the gods blocked the knowledge of death's approach.

"The animals know it, though. They know when death is approaching because they are in constant communion with the gods. But the gods no longer speak with men. In our sorrow and ignorance, our arrogance and vanity, we are the only creatures on earth who live out of communion with the higher levels. Only by living a pure life can we lift this curse from ourselves.

"So don't be afraid of death, Saihung. Rather, be prepared for its coming, know its approach, and seek the knowledge in this lifetime that will guide you to a higher reality in the next. Then, at the moment of death, you will cast off your body fearlessly and enter into the next cycle."

TEN

Immortals

EVEN AS SAIHUNG continued to learn from nature, he was fascinated and inspired by the Taoists of Huashan, men who embodied the art that Saihung was only beginning to acquire. Their Taoism was as individual as their personalities and inclinations. They exemplified China's and Taoism's reclusive tradition, because they had isolated themselves from the mundane world's illusions and pitfalls to perfect their art and seek higher knowledge. Neither wealth, fame, family, nor official position meant anything to them. They were hermits for whom the vanity of the world was all too gossamer.

Taoist recluses in particular had probably existed since antiquity. Some lived anonymously in mist-shrouded valleys. Others made great social contributions, but still essentially were of the same traditions, because their work was always the product of inward investigation. Huang Di, the Yellow Emperor, wrote the *Classic of Internal Medicine*, still used today. Shen Nong experimented on himself with thousands of herbs, his "stomach-with-a window" being a metaphor for his meditative abilities. Fu Xi invented the *Ba Gua* diagram that was the basis of the *I Ching* and divination. Hua Tuo perfected the art of surgery and the Five Animals therapeutic exercises. Lao Tzu and Chuang Tzu wrote important works. All these men, whether they passed through this world mysteriously or left great traces, were men who shunned the world for the sake of their science and art.

Unique among the Taoist recluses were men who sought immortality through internal alchemy. These hermits, like the legendary Ge Hong (Ko Hung), withdrew from the world in their quest for alchemical mixtures of gold and cinnabar, mercury and lead, that would grant them immortality and ascension into heaven. Taoists on Huashan still engaged in that quest, but unlike many of their predecessors, they had abandoned poisonous metallics in favor of *qigong*, herbs, and meditation.

Some of the masters of Huashan were already addressed as "Immortal." These were highly regarded individuals, ageless in appearance. Their titles meant "realized persons," signifying that the masters had fulfilled, as a minimum requirement, the completion of internal alchemy for the sake of longevity, liberation from the cycle of transmigration, enlightened perception of the nature of life, astral travel, and the total memorization of the hundreds of volumes comprising the Taoist canon. So accomplished were the Immortals that they were exempt even from the Grand Master's authority. He knew they were above him in their achievements.

The Grand Master was keeping Saihung by his side for longer periods of time. Saihung served his master by combing his hair, washing his feet, preparing his calligraphy paper, or carrying his medicine box during travels. It was both an opportunity for the Grand Master to observe Saihung subtly, and for Saihung to learn from the Grand Master's own way of life. Being a companion to his master led to unique introductions to the high masters of Huashan.

Saihung met the first of Huashan's immortals one afternoon when he had gone to find his master on an upper terrace of the temple. Saihung ran up happily to him.

"Gong-Gong! Gong-Gong!" he called, addressing his master as if he were a grandfather. "Here I am!"

The Grand Master turned and smiled, placing a hand on the little boy.

"Gong-Gong, I've got some new 'mouse songs' to whisper in your ear. Just like my uncles here, I learn from the animals too! Listen!"

The Grand Master bent down and Saihung sang his song. His master laughed with pleasure.

"That's a very nice song, Saihung," said the Grand Master when Saihung had finished.

"I've got more!" said Saihung excitedly.

"Perhaps later," replied the Grand Master. "Right now, I need to go and meet someone."

"Is Uncle Yang, the Taiji Master, coming back?"

"No, Saihung. This is someone you've never met before."

Master and disciple walked for over an hour until they came to a tiny stucco cottage. It was plain, with only a few square windows and an old tile roof. It was summer, and every building on Huashan had its windows propped open to admit the warm sunlight. The windows of this one, however, were tightly shut. The door was slightly ajar and, after knocking, the two stepped inside.

The small interior was very dark and quiet, and a flow of cool air blew on them as they entered. Still blind from the bright sun, Saihung's vision adjusted slowly. After a while he saw that, set among a few modest furnishings, a low square table, and a gourd, was a large coffin.

Saihung saw his master drop down to his hands and knees, and Saihung automatically followed. He was puzzled. He had only seen his master bow during ceremonies. But there was no altar here, and his master couldn't be bowing to the coffin. Saihung completed his bow and looked up. There was a tall figure standing before them.

The figure remained standing and acknowledged their bow with a slight nod.

"Hey, you!" cried Saihung, "Why don't you bow, too? Don't you know how important my master is?"

"Saihung!" said the Grand Master sharply. "Don't be rude. He is the master here, not I." He turned to the man. "Greetings to the Bat Immortal."

The Bat Immortal smiled slightly. He was tall, thin, and moved in an almost feminine fashion. His face was small, his

The Bat Immortal

beard and hair braided with ribbons, his skin unwrinkled, pale, and bloodless. The eyes were sunken, the skin around them blackened, and they were almost closed all the time. But from the narrow slits of his eyes there seemed to shine an inner light, a hidden glow.

"I've come to ask a point about the scriptures," said the Grand Master.

The Bat Immortal acknowledged the request by stepping forward. He avoided the sunlight coming through the door, and his steps were soundless. He stopped in front of Saihung. His eyelids lifted slightly; the glow from his eyes intensified.

"Is this the boy you mentioned?" he asked in a thin and hollow voice.

"Yes," replied the Grand Master.

The Bat Immortal turned back to Saihung. Saihung looked up and he had the uncanny feeling that the Bat Immortal gazed directly through his eyelids. Saihung's attention lapsed and when he again became aware, the Bat Immortal had turned away.

The Grand Master sent Saihung outside to wait.

When he emerged an hour later, the Grand Master walked directly away. Saihung followed him. After a half-hour of silence, the Grand Master told him about the Bat Immortal.

"The Bat Immortal practices extreme yin training. That's why he has taken the name he has and sleeps in a coffin, avoids sunlight, stays only in cold places, and never eats anything hot. He cultivates the Great Yin, and this is the source of his spirituality."

"He seems like a wicked man, with those dark circles and ghostly movements," said Saihung.

"Don't think he is evil," cautioned his master. "He frightens you because he is an unfamiliar person. Naturally. He is immortal, and immortals are rarely glimpsed."

"But Gong-Gong, I don't understand why you bow to him. Everyone always bows to you."

"Saihung, there are always greater and greater masters, and we must always show our respect."

"Why is he great?"

"The Bat Immortal is one of the premier authorities on the scriptures. He can elucidate any point of the entire Taoist canon. In fact, he has all the scriptures committed to his infallible memory."

Saihung thought of the hundreds of scriptures he had had to air out and all the memorization he had to do in school. He did not like that kind of Taoism.

"But Gong-Gong, don't you know the scriptures already?"

"My understanding is very far below the Bat Immortal's. Taoists must learn continually. When they need instruction, they must seek it out.

"Let me explain. When we assigned you to care for the greenhouse, you knew nothing about it. You had to use your own initiative and ask many people for instructions, didn't you?"

Saihung agreed.

"In the same way, even the masters must work to dispel their own ignorance. We are all seekers of knowledge, and we must all perfect our knowledge. On Huashan, there is always an answer. If we need guidance, we ask an old master. If he does not know, there is always an older one still."

Saihung was later introduced to two immortals who not only had two different ways of seeking their knowledge but also shared it with other masters on Huashan through public discourses. The two lived in another small shrine and were paired together. They were known as the Yin-Yang Immortals.

On the occasion of one of their lectures, the Grand Master brought Saihung into their shrine. The two sat upon a platform side by side. One was small and dark and sat with closed eyes. The other was large and light-skinned and gazed out at the gathering audience with a piercing look.

"What an odd pair!" Saihung exclaimed.

"You turtle's egg!" scolded his master as he slapped the back of Saihung's head. "Be more respectful!"

Saihung rubbed his head and took a second look at the youthful-looking Yin-Yang Immortals.

Yin did not look at all Chinese. He was very dark-skinned. His black hair, though coiled in a topknot, was wavy. His uncut beard was curly. He sat crosslegged in loose gray robes; a white cord from his left shoulder encircled his body diagonally. Saihung had never seen such a person before. It was not until Saihung visited India years later that he recognized the Yin Immortal's ancestry and accent.

Yang, on the other hand, was tall, robust, and ruddy-skinned. He had thick, straight, coiled, jet-black hair, and a massive shaven face. His gray robes were almost bursting because of the muscles of his deep chest. On closer scrutiny, Saihung remembered having seen the Yang Immortal striding Huashan's cliff paths with sure and mighty steps.

The Grand Master explained to Saihung that the Yin-Yang Immortals were peerless in expounding the constantly shifting course of the Tao, but that they experienced it in two different modes. The Yin Immortal was the master of inner Taoism. He explored innermost consciousness through days of deep meditation and returned to report his discoveries. The Yang Immortal experienced outer Taoism. In his walks around the mountain, he observed all the phenomena and changes in the stars, nature, and weather, giving detailed lectures on things to come. Both of them combined their specialties with a solid foundation in the scriptures. Coupled together, the Yin-Yang Immortals elucidated and continued to explore further the entire range of Taoist knowledge.

The seminar was about to begin and the Grand Master, after introducing Saihung to the Yin-Yang Immortals, sent Saihung away with the two acolytes. "One should never rush in entering Taoism," said the Grand Master as he sent them away "One must proceed step by step, never advancing to the next stage until one is ready. One need not fret. If one discharges one's tasks and proceeds with one's training perseveringly, then the transitions are virtually automatic. You are young, Saihung. For now, it is enough for you to know that such people as the Yin-Yang Immortals exist."

Walks could be long and tiring for Saihung, for his master was tall, energetic, and long-legged, but the excursions always led to something educational. The Grand Master also pointed out things in nature, but they were quite different from those shown by the acolytes. Sometimes he would point to a trail and say, "There's a mystical palace at the end of that trail. Venture down and you will never return." At another time he paused by another trail and gestured toward the mist-shrouded ravine, saying, "This is the road to immortality."

And once he pointed out a lone Taoist with a lump on his head. "That is Master Sun the Immortal, who has seen many dynasties come and go."

Returning from one of their hikes on another occasion, the Grand Master led Saihung to the Pool of Heaven on the South Peak where a man squatted with his head tilted upward. This was perhaps the oddest immortal Saihung had seen. He was big and stout, and with his hands before him and head tilted back, he reminded Saihung of a frog. But the two acolytes had said that the frogs were meditating. This person seemed only to be sleeping. It did not seem to bother the Grand Master that the immortal appeared to be asleep. The Grand Master stood respectfully aside, hands folded, clearly prepared to wait. Saihung went closer to the massive figure. After several minutes he could contain himself no longer and shouted, "Hey! Hey, you! My master's here to see you! Why don't you wake up, you silly thing!"

"Saihung! You are disgraceful!" reprimanded his master.

"But, Gong-Gong! He's dead asleep and just squats there like a big lump. He's like a big toad, really. What an enormous toad he is! Hey, Gong-Gong, how will we cook such a large toad?"

"Saihung! Watch that saucy mouth of yours!"

Saihung crept right up to the figure. What a big head! It was wider at the jaws, and the face was flat. The nose was fat and bulbous, the thin-lipped mouth seemed almost to go from ear to ear, and the eyes were tightly shut. He was beardless, and his balding head looked all the more bullet-shaped.

"Why, he's quite asleep," said Saihung to himself. "I wonder if he'll feel this."

Saihung rapped his knuckles on the person's forehead. there was no response. He was about to try again when his master slapped him smartly on the back of his head.

"Behave, you turtle's egg!" roared the Grand Master.

"He always hits the same spot!" groaned Saihung softly, rubbing his head. But it seemed to be all right to look, if not to touch, and Saihung bent down again to examine the figure.

He was just about nose to nose when he was alarmed by the eyes opening and looking directly at him. The rubbery face took on an annoyed expression. Saihung jumped back hastily.

"Gong-Gong! He's awake! He's got green eyes!"

The Grand Master silently dropped down to his knees, and Saihung followed.

"Greetings to the Frog Immortal," saluted the Grand Master solemnly.

The Frog Immortal reluctantly acknowledged them with a gruff clearing of his throat. He contorted his face in a grimace of irritation, but soon seemed to fall back asleep. Long moments of silence followed.

"When a master has reached the stage he has," whispered the Grand Master to Saihung, "he has 'Immortal Spirit'—complete obliteration of the self and sensory awareness. He is in total union with the spiritual. The Frog Immortal has reached the highest stage of Taoism through the advanced practice of *qigong* and meditation. He is one with the void. He appears to be asleep because he is in a constant state of realization."

Presently, the Frog Immortal opened his eyes again. The Grand Master bowed and said, "Immortal, this is my disciple."

The Frog Immortal seemed to ruminate and then sprang

The Frog Immortal

away in a twenty-foot leap, landing in the same frog position. He paused a while and sprang back, landing lightly and soundlessly right before a startled Saihung. He scrutinized Saihung closely, and grunted.

"Did you come all this way to see me?" he asked temperamentally.

"Yes, Immortal," replied Saihung hesitantly.

"Hmmmmph! You don't understand this."

"It does look odd."

"Odd!" roared the Frog Immortal indignantly. "Odd! This is my meditation! I can leap so high because my body is filled with *qi*! I can make it lighter than air. Then I meditate beside water, or even on a wooden disc floating on the water. Water is my element. It has electricity. The body has electricity. Outer electricity excites inner electricity. Do you understand?"

"Yes, Immortal."

"No, you don't!" shouted the Frog Immortal. Saihung looked back innocently. The immortal was agitated for a moment, but then seemed to relent a bit. "Well, kid, maybe I'll teach you a thing or two someday," he muttered; then he fell motionless again.

It wasn't long before Saihung thought he felt the influence of the Frog Immortal as well as the Yin-Yang and Bat immortals. They appeared to him regularly in dreams, speaking things that Saihung could never recall. He felt that they somehow guided him. He questioned the two acolytes but they didn't know. Saihung asked his master whether the immortals could really appear in his dreams, but the Grand Master only turned his back abruptly and walked silently away.

ELEVEN

The Grand Master of Huashan

EVEN THOUGH Saihung's relationship with his master had grown as close as that of grandchild to grandfather, the Grand Master remained an awesome figure of authority and wisdom. He was kind and patient, but he could also be stern and strict. The Grand Master, like all Chinese patriarchal figures, raised Saihung with an absolutely firm hand, directing each stage of growth with a consistent eye to developing all of his ward's potential. Just as he allowed no questioning of his authority, he allowed no questioning of his personal background. Because he was a Taoist master, his own activities and history were not to be discussed. But it was natural that his disciples would be curious about him and, in their admiration, remember stories about him. If Saihung wanted to know more about his master, he had to ask many people and observe the Grand Master closely. The Grand Master, for his part, said nothing about his birth, age, learning, travels, or even where he went when he disappeared, sometimes for months, without any advance notice.

The only thing Saihung thought could be certain was something his mysterious "Gong-Gong" told him: that he had been reared on Huashan. But Saihung was surprised when, in talking to an old monk, he found that the Grand Master had come from elsewhere.

The two were working in the temple kitchen, and Saihung was chattering about his master.

"Gong-Gong says he was raised from a little boy right here on the mountain and that he's already ninety!"

"Shhh!" hushed the old monk. "Don't let him know we're talking about him."

"But Gong-Gong's far away."

"No! No! He'll know! Don't you know by now? The masters here can know anything!"

He motioned Saihung to a deep corner of the kitchen, near the great sacks of rice and the lines of dried herbs and vegetables. He glanced nervously around before leaning down. "Don't ever tell your master I told you this, but he came from another place."

"He did? Are you sure?"

"*I* was one of the boys raised on Huashan, and look at me now: gray and thin. When your master came here, his hair was already white. I was just twenty then. Now I've grown old, but your master's appearance remains the same.

"They said that *Da Shi* has been all over China, even to India, Tibet, and Persia. No one knows all his exploits, either as a Taoist or a martial artist, but he must have wandered for decades."

The old monk was whispering so softly by now that his face was nearly pressed to Saihung's. "Remember," he said in low tones, "don't ever reveal that you learned this from me. Your master will be truly angry with me if he finds out."

Saihung next questioned the two acolytes.

"How do I know Gong-Gong's really a Taoist master?" asked Saihung.

"The same way you recognize any master," replied Mist Through a Grove. "A master is someone who has answered many questions for himself and can answer any question for the student. He must be able to prove all he claims. He must practice what he preaches—and it should show. He should be in perfect health, with bright, clear eyes and such an attractive aura that you find yourself wanting just to be close to him. Finally, a master unselfishly teaches and helps his student, and there seems to be no end to what he can teach you. That is a master."

"But all I see Gong-Gong do is walk around," objected Saihung.

"You don't know, Saihung," said Sound of Clear Water. "He has great ability, only he veils it with humility."

"What's that?"

"Something you haven't learned yet," laughed Mist Through a Grove.

"I'll tell you some stories about the Grand Master, though," said Sound of Clear Water.

"His *qinggong* is very strong," he recounted. "It was a festival day and many pilgrims had come to the North Peak Temple. It had been raining, and the rock was wet. A little girl, playing at the edge, slipped and fell over a precipice.

"At that moment, *Da Shi* threw himself after her. He jumped down, seized her in midair, and cradling her gently, used his ability to land on a ledge forty feet below. He climbed back up and returned her safely to her mother."

"Later we saw *Da Shi* levitate," added Mist Through a Grove. "Every night for a certain duration of days, *Da Shi* meditates between 11 at night and 2 in the morning. The meditation builds up tremendous heat in the body. Our duty was to come in periodically, change the incense, and leave a gourd full of fresh spring water.

"We went quietly into his room. It was dark, and we did not see him. We glanced at his bed. It was empty. But then we looked up. *Da Shi* was sitting cross-legged in midair.

"We thought it might be some trick, and we passed our hands underneath. Brother even wanted to get his carpenter's rule and measure the height. But before he could go, *Da Shi* started laughing, and floated down. He called us turtle eggs and asked for water."

"So Gong-Gong's a sorcerer!" cried Saihung.

"No. No, he isn't a sorcerer. Such things are forbidden in our sect," said Mist Through a Grove. "You must understand this distinction. A sorcerer calls spirits from the other side to do his bidding. Each time, he barters part of himself until he is lost completely to evil. The Grand Master, however, can do what appears supernatural purely because of his spiritual advancement. His ability is a gift from the gods, not something bargained and gained from evil spirits.

"Did Gong-Gong explain how he levitated?" asked Saihung.

"No," replied Sound of Clear Water. "He's like that. He won't say. Even when we directly experienced his power, he wouldn't explain what had happened. *Da Shi* and we were on an herb-gathering trip in search of an herb that had the power to open all the body's energy pathways. We had to get it before the animals did—for they use it as medicine, too—and we had to go at twilight because this herb had a mystic glow visible only at dusk.

"It was early spring, and the runoff was heavy. A river we normally could ford was now swift with rushing water and splintered logs. Whenever we crossed a river, we always carried *Da Shi* but now we were sure that we'd be swept away.

"*Da Shi* pushed by us as we stood deliberating, and faced the river. In the twilight, he seemed even more mysterious. He cried out for us to follow, telling us to step where he stepped. He was testing our faith. We followed without hesitation.

"In the darkness we saw a beam of light shoot out from *Da Shi*'s back and connect to our navels. We were soaked, but there was no force from the water and all the logs avoided us. When we reached the other side, we eagerly questioned him, but *Da Shi* wouldn't discuss it. Still, we both remember vividly that beam of light sustaining us against the angry river."

The Grand Master was an accomplished martial artist and a member of the martial world. He had a private training hall in the temple grounds. Before long, Saihung began sneaking over to observe the Grand Master's practice.

The Grand Master began his practice sessions first with standing meditations that built up his internal energy. These were a series of static postures using different stances and hand gestures. After doing basic stretches and loosening exercises both to disperse the concentration of energy accumulated during the meditation and also to limber up, the Grand Master practiced acrobatics.

Fighting in China had reached such an accomplished level that somersaults, tumbling, high spinning jumps, and twisting flips were all part of a martial artist's repertoire. They could be used offensively or defensively. Cartwheels and handsprings could provide escapes from bone locks or weapons, while spinning and rolling added momentum to attacks. Combined with striking and kicking, acrobatics made the Grand Master even more formidable.

Tall, thin, over six feet in height but weighing only 130 pounds, he performed his gymnastics in breathtaking alternation with his fighting techniques. Roundhouse, jump, and crescent kicks were a blur of speed. Forward kicks swung to perpendicular. Combinations of kicks came in a successive flurry before his leg came down again. Palms, fists, elbows, chops, and thrusts came in rapid sequence.

The Grand Master's favorite hand techniques were palm attacks. Internal energy issued forth from his palms at the moment of impact, breaking bones, and rupturing organs without damaging the opponent's skin. He knew five different styles of palm fighting: the Butterfly, Willowleaf, Yin-Yang, Thunder, and Five Element Palms. During his nocturnal practice, the Grand Master practiced each style and their inspiration was immediately identifiable. The Butterfly Palms fluttered in unison attacks. The Willowleaf Palms twisted like blown leaves. Yin-Yang Palms attacked above and below in alternation. The Thunder Palms were straight lightning attacks, using the waist as a pivot. The Five Element Palm drew its energy from the psychic centers and was swiftest of all. When he had reached the peak of his practice, the Grand Master was a whirling tornado.

The Grand Master constantly received challenges, and he never failed to respond. He went to the designated place, defeated his opponent, and returned with no fanfare.

Challenges could take many different forms, but chief

among them were simple challenges of competition wherein the victor was required to heal the loser, or death matches where participants implicitly accepted the consequences. The matches were often held on high, unfenced platforms at least ten feet above the ground. Falls from such heights were dangerous and often fatal. The participants needed *qinggong* to leap up to the platforms, and this requirement barred unaccomplished fighters from participating.

Moreover, the platforms could in themselves present an added element to the match. Sometimes challengers fought on a 4-foot-square tabletop set with inverted tea cups. The fighters had to stay consistently on the cups or risk automatic disqualification. At other times, the fighters were on Plum Blossom Piles: forty-nine wooden posts, each 10 feet high, set in a plum blossom pattern and surrounded by upturned swords on the ground below.

One of the most unusual platforms was used in a challenge to the Grand Master. Saihung had not been permitted to attend the challenge because of his youth but had afterward heard a report from the acolytes. The Grand Master, as usual, had simply returned wordlessly and gone to his chambers.

Some months before, the Grand Master had heard of five Taoist priests in Sichuan Province who were violating the precepts. They were called the Five Poison Taoists and had not only taken concubines, but had also engaged in pimping, drug and slave trafficking, smuggling, and gambling. The Grand Master had openly denounced them and threatened to report them to the government if they did not reform.

The Five Poison Taoists had responded with a formal challenge. The Grand Master accepted, stipulating that the match had to be held at the base of Huashan, because, "I don't want you stinking up this sacred place."

The challengers sent men to build a dueling platform. At the base of the North Peak, they erected a circle of eight 20-foot poles with a radiating pattern of ropes. The platform was a gigantic spider web.

The Grand Master went to the challenge dressed in his regular white robes and carrying his only weapon, a throwing net. Dressed in black, with faces green from the toxins they used, the Five Poison Taoists stood defiantly on the posts. The Grand Master jumped immediately to the center of the web, and the fight began.

The Five Poison Taoists attacked, using patterns derived from the *Ba Gua*, and either charged in unison or attacked singly. The Grand Master did not want the fight to go on long, so he dealt with his opponents quickly. The eldest attacked with the symbol of Taoist priesthood, the horsehair whisk. He whipped it around in a lethal slice. But the Grand Master caught it with his net and dealt a mighty kick. His opponent staggered forward, blowing a jet of green poison. The Grand Master shielded himself with his sleeve and threw his opponent to the ground.

Now the Grand Master rushed forth and split the remaining fighters apart. Balancing nimbly on the ropes, he faced two men, one armed with a poisoned steel brush, the other with mirrored discs that reflected light into the Grand Master's eyes. The Grand Master caught the first man, but the second threw a disc and severed part of the net. Quickly, the Grand Master leapt forward and, by striking the arm of the imprisoned man, shot his steel brush into the disc fighter.

The last two fighters carried a folding fan with poisoned needles and twin spear-headed maces. The mace wielder was powerful and sought to smash the Grand Master's arms before thrusting at pressure points. With a high spinning leap, the Grand Master dodged not only his attack but also a dozen flying needles thrown from the fan. A single mid air kick into the throat of the fan fighter killed him, and the net brought the mace wielder to the ground as the Grand Master jumped from the platform.

Saihung was disappointed to hear about the fight only second hand, but one afternoon, when he was assisting his master at calligraphy, he had a personal opportunity to see the Grand Master fight.

Saihung laboriously ground the ink stick with water until it became a dark, thick liquid, and prepared the long accordion-folded paper. As the Grand Master formed his ideographs, Sai-hung guided the paper down the long, high table to dry before folding it at the end. He was fascinated to watch his master's smooth cursive as paper, brush, water, and ink, so mute before, became expressive trails.

The doors to the chamber burst open, and two young men charged in. They had managed to evade everyone between the North and South peaks and had found the Grand Master's chambers. The first man, dressed in purple with an orange sash and head cloth, carried a double-edged sword. The second, dressed in crimson with a black sash and head cloth, carried a large steel mace with a head eighteen inches in diameter. The swordsman addressed the Grand Master arrogantly:

"We've come for a certain manual on martial technique, and we know you are its custodian."

"Hand it over. You're an old man," the other added, "so we won't harm you unless you resist."

The Grand Master calmly put his brush down, carefully holding his trailing sleeve away from the still wet calligraphy.

"Nothing in life is easy," he said. "If you want it so much, come and get it. If your stars are right and I am to die today, then you'll have the manual. But if your stars are unfavorable, then I can guarantee you'll be reincarnated today."

The Grand Master's face took on a suddenly fierce look. He wound his trailing sleeves up in three quick circles. Rolling over the desk he landed right before them and unfurling his sleeves, insultingly slapped the faces of both his attackers with the whipping cloth.

The one in purple recovered quickly and thrust his sword forward. The Grand Master evaded; wrapping his sleeves around the sword blade, he trapped it. A single kick propelled the man crashing through the lattice windows.

The second one charged. The Grand Master sidestepped the mace and allowed his opponent's body to collide with his. The man seemed to be helplessly stuck to the Grand Master. The

Grand Master looked at him face to face and laughed tauntingly, just before he used a single palm blow to crumple his opponent.

Attracted by the commotion, the two acolytes came in and dragged the pair away. Saihung rushed forward from beneath the desk, a dozen questions readily falling from lips. Typically, the Grand Master remained silent and strode from the room.

Turning Point at Twelve

O N SAIHUNG's twelfth birthday, the Grand Master called him to his chambers. Three years on Huashan had changed him greatly. Saihung was less stubborn and talkative, and trusted his master's wisdom. The acolytes had encouraged his eagerness to learn, saying that he must seize every opportunity the Grand Master presented. Saihung went to see his master expectantly and the Grand Master spoke freely. It was time for Saihung to make a decisive commitment to his training.

"One's life proceeds in stages according to the twelve celestial stems," said the Grand Master. "People believe a person is shaped by upbringing or by society. In actuality, it is the seasons, the constellations, and fate that shape a person. Life is preordained by heaven; your destiny is to live out your span on this earth, but you must still make choices. Throughout your life, you will be confronted with decisions and challenges. This is how heaven will test you. How will you respond?

"A person is like a cartwheel; each stage of his life is like a spoke. When the wheel hits a rock, it will either stop, shatter, or roll right over. But the rock cannot be avoided. So it is for you: no matter what happens, you must meet life head on.

"You must proceed from one stage to another, just as the spokes of the cartwheel revolve. At each stage, you will experience new knowledge. It is only by using this knowledge and following uninterruptedly the turning of your life that you will fulfill your destiny.

"You may feel sad when it's time to go on. Emotion is natural. But it is right to go on, to change, to avoid stagnation. Feel no regrets. It is like the rattle you brought to this mountain. At

one time, you would not part with it. Now it has been left behind. Another day you will forsake other things of your boyhood, but neither you nor those things need be sad, for it is right that you grow.

"At the edge of each new phase, you will feel aspiration, curiosity, inquisitiveness. You will want knowledge, and acquiring some will only make you thirst for more. That is right. You are a human being, and it is human nature to seek knowledge. Therefore, pursue knowledge without hesitation or compromise.

"Remember, however, that the time to go from stage to stage is precise, just as the spokes of the cartwheel are precisely set. If you try to skip a stage, or rush to the next, your personality will warp. If you do not move on to the next stage, you will be retarded. The stages of growth can neither be avoided nor held fast. You must proceed through them. This requires guidance. Only a master can guide you, only he can perceive the stages, only he can shape you into the perfection you will need to succeed.

"Now, Saihung, you are a boy no longer. It is time for you to enter fully into your youth."

Thus, Saihung was sent to a dormitory in the South Peak monastery school, where he lived with many other students. Learning both from the exposure to other boys and the instruction of numerous teachers and often attending specialized classes in other temples, he nevertheless maintained his duties at the South Peak temple. Their responsibility and weight increased. Chopping wood, drawing well water, sewing and washing clothes, attending his master, and cooking were just some of his tasks. Saihung no longer played his pranks, nor did he resent his assignments. Everyone contributed to the temple, and he saw that only by cooperation could those in the monastery overcome the poverty and harshness of mountain life.

But the Grand Master gave Saihung a still deeper perspective of the importance of work. When Saihung brought dinner to the Grand Master one evening, the Grand Master expressed his approval, and explained his view.

"You once refused to do your chores. At other times you misbehaved. We denied you dinner. Now you understand. If you do not work, you do not eat. Work and reward go hand in hand.

"Everyone in the temple must work, and humility is always fostered. One who works, one who serves, cannot set himself above others. This is important, because with humility you will never become arrogant. No matter how high you climb on the path of knowledge, you will not misuse your powers but instead will help others. Through work and humility, you will know compassion.

"You will also be able to survive. If you descend the mountain and meet hardship, you must know how to provide for yourself. You will be able to take a job and have marketable skills. Work is an integral part of your training. It teaches you cooperation, humility, compassion, and skill. So work hard, Saihung, work."

Work was drudgery, but studying the classics and morality was far worse drudgery to Saihung. He attended school with a student body of 500 boys, all strictly controlled by the priests. Classes were signaled by the temple bell. At that time, each boy had to enter the classroom promptly, bow to a statue of Kong Ming, the Taoist strategist of the Three Kingdoms period, and take his place in the rows of students who sat cross-legged on the floor. The boys were forbidden to talk to one another or to look in any direction except straight ahead. The teachers sat on platforms and demanded absolute attention throughout tedious hours of reading, writing, history, geography, mathematics, classics, and morality.

Both the classics and Taoist scriptures were central to the curriculum. The Confucian texts were the *Four Books* and the *Five Classics*, which Saihung read, transcribed, recited, and discussed every day. Taoist books such as the *Jade Classic of the Yellow Chamber* laid out the theoretical foundations of Taoism.

Far from believing in any conflict between Confucianism and Taoism, the priests demanded perfect mastery of both schools' classics, stressing morality as a consistent theme.

"Don't lie," lectured the ethics teacher. "Why shouldn't you lie? The words of the sages are 'Wrong no one, lest others wrong you.' Take this as an example:

"Imagine that you are walking on Huashan during the night. You have a lantern, but a lost boy you meet doesn't have one. Out of mischief, you send him down the wrong path. The boy falls off a cliff and dies because you lied.

"Don't think evil things and you will not do wrong. People do bad things because they give in to temptation. But if we don't even think of temptation, if we do not even allow ourselves to consider it, we will not have anything to which to yield."

"That's easy to say," thought Saihung. If the temptation was there, it was there. He thought about the times back home when he tied his tutor's queue to the chair. . . .

"Saihung!" growled the teacher, "Are you thinking bad thoughts again?"

The teaching of ethics extended beyond the classroom. The temple was a closed, twenty-four-hours-a-day system. There were literally no temptations permitted. No outside influences contradicted the priests, and they, with their perfect realization and psychic abilities, could even read their students' thoughts and worked single-mindedly on raising them properly. They generally tried to teach by example and persuasion, but severely punished liars, cheaters, thiefs, and bullies by beating and, occasionally, expulsion.

Such strict supervision and rigorous academic standards brought up most of the students to be intelligent, precocious boys. Saihung with his latent talents, blossomed quickly. In response, the Grand Master returned to the theme of humility in his talks with Saihung.

"The more you learn, the more you must use your knowledge for others," said the Grand Master. "The wiser you become, the more unselfish you must also become. As your experience deepens, and with it your humility, you will realize unfathomable depths of knowledge. You can never become arrogant and narrow-minded if you perceive how small your abilities are when contrasted to those of the greatest.

"Remember to use your knowledge in the service of others, but expect nothing in return. Never seek a reward for your labors, for that is a sin."

THIRTEEN

Luohans, Herbs, and *Qigong*

T HE TAOISTS believed that the spiritual was rooted in the physical and that physical training was a prelude to internal alchemy. The mind and body were one. The mind existed not in the head but throughout the body in psychic centers. The body was the practitioner's base for transcendence, and it had to be made into a sound spiritual vehicle. The Grand Master explained the concepts thoroughly to Saihung.

"You were not always yourself and will not always remain yourself—'You' who are this physical body. You come into this world with problems and dilemmas to be solved either as punishment for transgressions in past lives or because you were unsatisfied in past lives. That is why you must meet all your problems and hindrances in this lifetime. Burn all your attachments to worldly goals, purge desire, satisfy the thirst for knowledge. Never refuse any experience; overcome all your obstacles. You can then leave this world fulfilled and go to a higher plane.

"This is called purging one's *ming huan*, one's karma, and to achieve this you must live in vital health as long as you need. You must ensure not only that you live to purge all consequences of your past lives, but also that you create no new difficulties. The proper method is to purify one's body, enter into the spiritual, and return to the void. The beginning is to train the body."

"*Da Shi*," Saihung said, addressing his master by title now that he was a full-fledged student, "Why do you stay? Haven't you achieved your liberation?"

"Some spiritual people leave the earth the moment they are free of their past acts. But the Taoists believe in preserving their knowledge and helping the next generation to succeed as well."

"So you could leave?"

"Maybe not," joked the Grand Master, his eyes crinkling with humor. "Maybe you're my curse."

Saihung reddened. "Really, *Da Shi?*"

The Grand Master laughed and patted Saihung comfortingly. "I teach you because it is my duty. I have a task in this lifetime. I'll depart only after it is accomplished."

"Do I have a task?"

"Of course you do."

"What is it?"

The Grand Master roared in amusement. "You're rushing. That is not for you to know yet. If you want to find out, you have to start at the beginning."

The physical training Saihung embarked on comprised three distinct parts. First was the 108 Luohans style, second was a regimen of diet and herbs, and third was *qigong*. Together they were intended to discipline Saihung in mind and body and tone his body structure to a high degree.

The 108 Luohans was a martial style that included calisthenics, making the body light, reflex training, self-defense, and solo sets. It was a rigorous system taking two years to learn. The Taoists on Huashan regarded its strenuous movements, emphasizing stretching, strength, coordination, and aerobic exercise, as ideal for young boys.

The 108 Luohans was a Buddhist system and had come to Huashan during the Tang dynasty when Hindu, Buddhist, and Taoist masters, uninterested in religious factionalism, had gathered together to exchange knowledge. Finding similarities between Kundalini yoga and Taoist meditation, the Taoist and Hindu masters intermingled the physical techniques even while retaining their allegiance to their respective gods. The Taoists taught the Buddhists blood-circulating meditation and internal exercises to counter the headaches and hemorrhoids caused by long periods of zazen (a sitting meditation). In turn, the Buddhists gave the Taoists their external martial art, the Luohan system.

The Luohan style began with calisthenic training. The 108 Luohans were Buddhist saints, and according to legend each had contributed one of the exercises. They were an ideal starting point for boys' training, for they were like playing. Capturing the imagination of the students with their imitative movements, the Luohan exercises were effective and fun.

"Can you imitate this? Can you imitate that?" Saihung's Luohan teacher usually challenged before introducing a new movement, and the boys always tried to meet his challenge. The "lizard" was an exercise moving the hands circularly and swiveling the hips, to keep the spine flexible while working the lungs. The "cat" involved leaning over, arms dangling, legs straight and trotting, to loosen the body and stretch the back and hamstrings. The "monkey" was a walking squat, back straight and arms at the sides, to strengthen the legs and cultivate balance. The "alligator" was to walk in a push-up position, using only the hands and dragging the feet to build up arm strength. By the time the boys had learned all 108 postures, they had exercised every muscle, bone, organ, and joint, and had thoroughly strengthened their circulation and stamina.

The next phase was making the body light. This skill was an asset not only for the tumbling and jumping of fighting, but for a spiritual reason as well. The Taoists believed that a light body not only was unburdened by the blockages, wastes, fat, accumulations, and toxins present in most people's bodies, but was also an important prerequisite for internal alchemy. The Luohan teachers interpreted this literally: they threw their students off cliffs.

The heights began at six feet and progressed up to fifteen feet during later training. Mats were placed at the bottom to cushion the fall, but with the teachers pushing the students off, the mats were not quite thick enough for comfort.

"Who will be first in this new training?" asked the teacher.

"I'll impress my classmates," Saihung thought, "and volunteer. They'll be jealous when I do it perfectly."

The teacher accepted Saihung's quick response with a knowing smile, and pushed Saihung without any preliminaries. Saihung plunged to the bottom amid wild laughter from his classmates. But their laughing soon gave way to soft moans as each of them got up at the bottom, rubbing bruised limbs.

The teacher constantly exhorted them to land on their feet. It was days before Saihung could do that, but he eventually managed it. When he could do every leap successfully for the duration of the class, he was beaming with pride.

The teacher grinned. He added a foot to the height. Who thought they could do it?

Saihung's hand was up again.

"Do you really think you can?"

"Yes."

"All right. This time put your hands in the praying position."

Saihung happily folded his hands.

"Prepare to jump . . ."

Saihung stationed himself confidently at the edge.

". . . and land on one foot."

Weeks later, winter had come on and the class moved to an indoor training hall. All the boys could now sail down drops of fifteen feet with ease. Now they were asked to jump off ordinary tables.

The boys all thought it would be easy, but they were surprised. They had become accustomed to the deep drops and the time they had, while falling, to find their balance. Now they found that after the teacher's shove they could not find their equilibrium in time.

Saihung eventually learned to land cross-legged and in one-legged postures and handstands, and to include flips and twists before the floor seemed to rush up swiftly to meet him. In the calisthenics phase, he had developed raw strength. Now he combined strength with speed, timing, and a light body to complete gracefully the second part of the Luohan training.

Reaction time was the third phase. This was a different kind of training from the acrobatic falls. In this phase, Saihung learned to evade or catch objects coming at him, to develop hand-eye coordination.

On the first day of this period, the boys were instructed to wear dark clothes. The teacher had a stick with a bag of chalk-dust at the end. The object was to evade the teacher's swings and thrusts, but it was difficult because the teacher was a master spearman. Saihung tried continually to have less than two chalk marks on his clothes.

They also participated in bean-bag catching. At first, it was a simple matter of catching a few bags. Soon it was a bewildering situation of catching several bags thrown by several teachers at once. The demanding exercise was made more difficult by the final stipulations of *how* to catch it. Saihung found himself exasperated by instructions to catch bags behind him, under his legs, or with only two fingers.

Self-defense training began with body-toughening exercise. The Luohan system was a "hard" style—one based on speed, muscular force, long-range kicks, and hard strikes. The teachers wanted the students to have a sound basis in fighting techniques, both for the sake of self-defense against bandits and animals as well as for physical discipline.

Body toughening started with the catching of large medicine balls. The teachers were strong, and they frequently knocked Saihung down, winding him. Although he was only thirteen, he soon grew used to even this new requirement and moved on to blocking. Instead of catching the medicine balls thrown at him, he blocked them with his forearm, shoulder, back, leg, and stomach.

Stance and footwork were the next level. All Chinese martial styles were solidly based on stances, and a large range of sophisticated leg positions were developed. The most basic was the horse stance, with the legs sunk in a stable bow-legged horse-riding stance. A Chinese martial artist's skill was only as good as his stance or *horse*. In a rushing river, where the resistance of the water developed greater strength in the legs, Saihung practiced shifting from one horse stance to another: bow, side, twisting, hanging, and crane stances.

Actual self-defense ability was learned only with a partner. "You've all seen sets—the solo exercise performance that reveals an art's trademark techniques," said the teacher. "But this is not how one learns self-defense. You must spar, in prearranged movements and freestyle, until you have thoroughly absorbed the techniques. Only after you've understood the styles' rationale do you go on to learn the set. Then mastery comes easily.

"Some styles are based on human movements, others on animal movements. The Luohan system includes both. But you cannot fight like an animal until you've learned to fight like a human. Again, self-defense, where you must relate to a partner, is the beginning point."

When he began to learn self-defense, Saihung finally appreciated all his previous training. Every blocking, punching, and kicking technique learned, every avenue of attack and defense explored, every movement practiced exhaustively, drew on the strength and balance he had already acquired. It was on the very firm foundation of his early training that Saihung perfected his budding martial ability.

After the torturous and bitter training of the first four stages, the final stage exhilarated him. In this stage he learned sets, series of fighting techniques that contained the hallmarks of a particular style. Performed in a continuous routine, sets featured such characteristic elements as heavy fists in the Luohan style or palm strikes in the Five Element palm style. Most sets also included a variety of other attacks, including seizing, slapping, straight punches, uppercuts, elbow strikes, and kicks. There could be any number of postures in a set, with some styles having a thousand movements in one set. Thus, besides teaching the rudiments of attack and defense, a set also built stamina, internal strength, and contributed to overall health.

Saihung whirled through the succession of each fierce posture with precise force and timing, displaying the powerful air
of a young warrior. He was confident that he had absorbed all
the training as he passed his final test. He was proud to have
gone the full course. The sets were so liberating, they became
almost a celebration dance.

At his graduation, Saihung went forth eagerly to receive the
comments of his teachers.

"Not bad," was all they would say. Even at the end they still
demanded that the student push on; therefore praise, the ultimate reward, was not yet appropriate.

In his conversations with the Grand Master, Saihung
learned that strenuous physical training was important at an
early age. The bones and muscles were still soft and pliable. It
was the ideal opportunity to shape his body and permanently
establish his external structure. Yet the cultivation of the internal structure was just as important. The temple provided vegetarian meals that were intended to keep Saihung calm, elated,
and clear. But the diet was insufficient to sustain harsh physical training. Saihung was given herbal teas every day that
complemented both his diet and exercise.

These tonic herbs, picked in the wilds, provided vitamins
and nutrients that were applicable to specific parts of the
body. The masters judged whether any part of Saihung's system needed strengthening and gave him powerful doses of
herbs that could increase his qi, increase muscle strength, keep
the bones pliable, feed his organs, open his meridians, cleanse
toxins, build his circulation, or meet any other problem. The
Taoist medical system was based on this tonification approach
as well as on a healing approach. First they strengthened the
body, then they refined it for optimum exertion.

Herbal tonics also integrated Saihung's body with each season. This was just one of the pragmatic manifestations of the
Taoist philosophy to live with the flow of the universe. According to their medical theory, each season acted on the body
in certain ways and typically damaged specific organs. The

body had to be prepared for each season by cleansing it of any bad effects from the last one and preparing it for the coming one.

Unfortunately, medical theory and philosophy had not yet yielded a palatable approach. The hot herbal solutions were thick, black as coffee, and often unbearably bitter. Saihung always felt stronger and more energetic after taking them, so he readily recognized their indispensable value. But he hated the taste, and took every opportunity to complain to the Grand Master.

"These herbs are important," responded his master. They will transform your body. After you complete your training, your body will be unlike an average person's."

"But do I have to drink the herbs?"

"Of course you do!" laughed the Grand Master. He leaned over. "You know, Saihung, many of the old masters eat no solid food at all. They want to make their bodies light enough to go to heaven, so they only eat herbs."

Saihung wondered if liberation was important enough for him to endure a lifetime of awful-tasting herbs. But he had to acknowledge their efficacy. He had even liked them when his master, in a light-hearted and conspiratorial way, had given him brain tonics to help him pass his examinations. Even without seeking immortality, Saihung decided that herbs could be of mortal value.

The Luohan training and herbs complemented *qigong*. *Qigong* directed the body's vital energy, increased its storage of *qi*, and also contributed to opening the meridians.

The Grand Master explained it to Saihung:

"In the beginning of the universe, only *qi*—pure life force—existed. *Qi* coagulated into the Five Elements—metal, water, wood, fire, and earth. The Five Elements combined into Yin and Yang. Yin and Yang created humanity. Yin and Yang combined further to become the Grand Ultimate—*Tai Ji. Tai Ji* became *Wu Ji*—Nothingness. Nothingness became Stillness. Then the entire process reversed itself, and began again. The

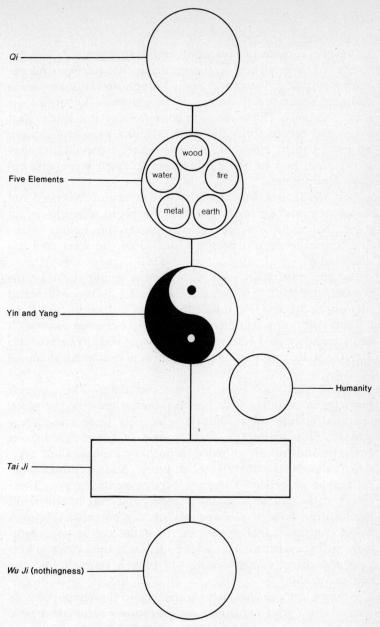

Progression of qi to Wu Ji

universe is constantly expanding and contracting.

"We are microcosms of the universe. We recreate this sequence in *qigong*. First your *jing* is brought to the solar plexus and unites with breath—the *qi* of the universe—to become the *qi* of your body. The *qi* drops to your *dan tian*, just below your navel, and becomes yin and yang. Yin and yang rise straight up to the third eye—the psychic center between the eyebrows—and become the ultimate, spirit. Spirit ascends to become Nothingness.

"We are Taoists. But where does Tao begin? We need not search near and far for it. Tao does not begin somewhere 'out there,' but right here, in the solar plexus. Tao begins in the first union between a person's individual life force and the universal *qi*.

"So you must train your *qi*. You must gather it. You must ensure a constant flow and storage of vital *qi*. You will feel it fill your body. You will inhale the whole universe.

"You then must also direct it. *Qi* is the universal essence. It can strengthen and heal any part of your body. The postures direct it so that no part of your body is ever starved or cut off from *qi*.

"Third, you must open all your meridians. The universe flows on uninhibitedly. A person's energy must do the same. Originally, humanity's energy channels were completely opened. Human beings were capable of flight, prodigious strength, and psychic knowledge. But they misused their abilities. The gods place three gates on every person as punishment for human perversity. These three gates are on the spinal meridian at the tailbone, shoulderblades, and base of the skull, limiting the flow of *qi* and blocking our potential. Through *qigong*, you must shatter each of the gates, before your pathways will open throughout your body. Only then can you harness and direct enough energy to launch yourself into the spiritual realm."

Saihung and his classmates were sent to the temple of a *qigong* master, who explained each posture's rationale before

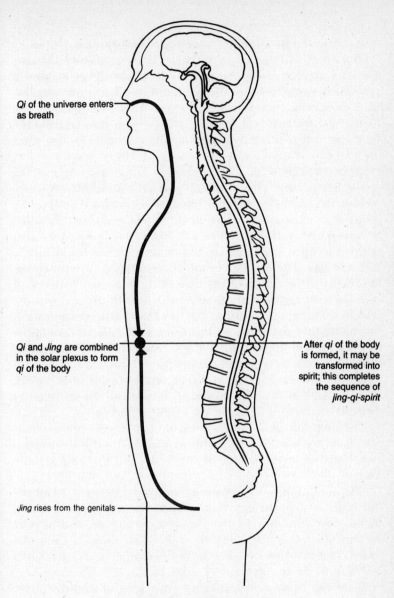

Qi of the universe enters as breath

Qi and *Jing* are combined in the solar plexus to form *qi* of the body

After *qi* of the body is formed, it may be transformed into spirit; this completes the sequence of *jing-qi-spirit*

Jing rises from the genitals

Formation of the body's qi

demonstrating it. Saihung learned one posture a week until he had mastered the entire set of 108. *Qigong* increased his lung capacity, deepened his chest, neutralized pain from his severe martial training, and, as the Grand Master had promised, began to open his meridians and break the three gates. At the end of the the two-year training, the *qigong* master selected ten postures suited to each practitioner to maintain his body for life.

Qigong began with the tying of a large sash around the waist. There were several reasons for this. First, the sash supported the organs against the tremendous pressure built up by successive inhalations—one posture, for example, included thirteen inhalations before exhaling. Secondly, the sash helped to open the front channel running from the throat to the *dan tian*. There could be no success without its opening. Normally the *qi* followed the flow of the blood and organs on a downward zigzag path. Binding the sash forced it down the single center channel to the *dan tian* rather than permitting it to sink to the anus. Only by breathing to the *dan tian* could the energy then be channeled to the sacrum, and enter the spine. Finally, the sash facilitated the distribution of *qi* during movement to the four limbs. As *qi* was generated in the solar plexus, the pressure of the sash forced it outward to the extremities instead of allowing it to remain in the abdomen.

The first posture aimed directly at opening the center channel. Saihung learned a pigeon-toed stance with the arms pressing together at the center of the body and the chin on the chest.

"Pay attention to this posture," said the teacher. "It embodies important principles. First, notice the locks. Head, chest, hands, legs, and toes, by their inward contraction, seal in your energy. Round your shoulders, raise the spine, depress the chest. This is called *han xiong ba bei;* it empties your chest, sinks the energy to the *dan tian*. Exhale to the *dan tian*. Swallow. Release the pressure by clicking your tongue slightly. After two years, your swallow will plunge straight to the *dan tian*.

There will be physical evidence of this. You will hear rumbling in your abdomen when you swallow through the opened channel, and you will have an actual line, a real channel, visible on the skin surface.

"In *qigong*, as in all Taoist training, you must search for the confirmatory signs. When you do *qigong*, you must feel heat all over your body. This is the energy. When you direct it to an organ—the spleen, for instance—you must feel both heat and vibration, concentrated at that one point. If you do not feel these signs, you are practicing incorrectly and will not only miss the benefits but will also be injured.

"*Qigong* practitioners are extremely concerned about injury. Erroneous practice will lead to chest pains, nausea, dizziness, vomiting, and hemorrhaging. Do the postures carefully, breathe deeply, and concentrate your mind to direct the energy."

After each posture, a neutralization movement released excess *qi* to prevent such injury. The practitioner inhaled unusual amounts of *qi*, and it obviously had to be let out instead of being trapped in the body. The neutralization was a forcible exhalation, a rolling of the shoulders to dislodge air pockets trapped in the lungs, a deep inhalation, and a final exhalation.

The first *dan tian*-swallow posture and the neutralization were the beginning and end of each posture, and framed within them were postures with a wide range of purposes. Their names were self-explanatory: Gathering the *Qi*, Expelling the Toxins, *Qi* to the Skin, *Qi* to the Four Limbs, *Qi* to the Heart, *Qi* to the Lungs, *Qi* to the Diaphragm. There were postures that toned all the organs and viscera. Others, such as the *Qi* to the Nasal Passages, were cleansing exercises. Some, such as Opening the Eight Psychic Meridians, connected and purged the entire meridian system. In total, the 108 postures covered every possible need.

All ailments the practitioner had were corrected over the two years. The teacher explained that the postures could also cure many chronic diseases. *Qi* to the Prostate Gland prevented or alleviated the common swelling of that gland. The Walking Dog Step pumped blood to the loins, preventing cancer of the colon. *Qi* to the Bones mitigated against rheumatism. *Qi* to the Head alleviated nervous disorders, neurasthenia, and poor memory.

Qigong, herbs, and the Luohan style all functioned on both a spiritual and a physical level. They truly united mind and body as one, and prepared the totality of Saihung's personality for higher stages. He found himself feeling different. What ordinary people regarded as good health was now something inconceivable to him. Now he knew Taoist health, with every organ related to the earth itself, every meridian paralleling the pathways of the stars, every movement revolving like the planets. His body was purified, his mind clear, and he had attained true balance.

PART THREE

MARTIAL WANDERINGS
AND
MEDITATION

FOURTEEN

Wudangshan

Iₙ HIS EARLY TEENS, Saihung be-
gan traveling extensively to learn from martial artists. "These
men have something unique," said his master. "They are master fighters, but they are dying without anyone else reaching
their stature. You must study with them now. Boxing will im-
prove both your spirituality and fighting."

The influence of both the Grand Master and Guan Jiuyin,
men famous and highly respected in the martial world, en-
abled Saihung to study with many great teachers. Martial arts
excited him passionately, almost becoming more important
than Taoism, and he often entered provincial tournaments.
His boxing teachers guided him strictly, and he learned both
in private and in classes. An important place to which he journeyed was Wudangshan, the center of Taoist martial arts in
China.

Wudangshan was the sacred mountain of the Pole Star Sect
of Taoism; internal alchemy combined with martial arts was
their specialty. For centuries, great boxers and spiritual men
had emerged from its seventy-two peaks, including Zhang
Sanfeng, the fourteenth-century creator of Taijiquan, and Bai
Mei, the nemesis of Shaolin. Wudang styles were supremely
effective, and Saihung learned from four main teachers.

The four masters were not priests but fighters who had tak-
en refuge on Wudangshan. Seeking spiritual redemption, they
came to the mountain to learn Taoism in repentance for their
years of killing in the martial world. In return for the mercy of
the Taoist priests, the Iron Luohan, Crane, Monkey, and Snake
masters taught their arts to the students.

The Iron Luohan master was in his forties, and was a compe-
tent and accomplished boxer. A member of the Shaolin tradi-

tion, he had enormous muscles and an idealistic temperament. Wanting very much to identify with the image of a heroic knight, he was a paragon of chivalry and always championed the causes of the weak. Many martial artists looked down on him, for they were interested only in the practice of killing, and were not idealistic, weak, or compassionate. But the Iron Luohan master maintained his principles and sought to teach his students heroic aspiration as well as his boxing system.

The Iron Luohan system—consisting of several styles: Tam Family style, Long Fist, Iron Wire Fist, and the Eighteen Luohan Fist—emphasized muscular strength. The master taught that all the body should be as tough and hard as iron and that the most critical part of training was the forearms. Unless the forearms or "bridge hands," were toughened, blocks were ineffective, grappling was weak, and punches lacked power. Training the bridge hands was excruciating. With his arms straight at the sides, Saihung lay on two chairs that supported only his head and heels as progressively heavier sandbags were added to his wrists. Then he had to whip through sets with extensive jumping, stretching, springing, crisp blocks, and power punches. Only with this grueling daily training did the Iron Luohan master feel the students could achieve the proper degree of hard strength.

The Crane master was an extremely thin man in his fifties. His long face with a pointed chin held two inquisitive eyes with irises so large that almost no white showed. He had thin black hair braided into a queue. His arms were like stalks, and he walked like a crane, in a long-legged, toed-out, syncopated gait.

The White Crane style made extensive use of qi and posture. Balance and energy circulation were essential. In contrast to the Iron Luohan master's emphasis on muscular strength, the Crane master urged the students to inflate their limbs with qi to achieve the same effect. If that were done, he said, one need rely only on posture to win a fight.

The master personally proved his point in endless sparring

sessions. Saihung, confident in his Luohan training, went forward. But to his frustration, he was unable to strike the master, who never blocked but only evaded, in a succession of beautiful birdlike poses. Sometimes he looked like a flying crane, and at other time, he eluded Saihung with one-legged postures.

"The crane is a bird," lectured the master. "Birds are proud and arrogant. They strike poses. Show off. This is the characteristic of the style. Your opponent attacks, but you are interested only in maintaining your best profile. Let him attack. You need only move into your posture. If his arms get caught in your 'wing,' if your 'beak' strikes him, it is from your posture, not from a premeditated effort."

The Crane master soon showed his devastating attacks. He favored the Crane Fist, a beaklike formation of the thumb and fingertips pointed together. The strike was sophisticated. All the force was directed onto a small area, increasing its impact. The attacks came from unexpected angles in a battery of bewildering hooks and zig-zag strikes. The Crane master could abruptly change directions and always succeeded in penetrating Saihung's defenses to peck at eyes, ears, throat, or pressure points.

The Monkey master was a clown. Seldom serious, he laughed and chattered constantly. Living in a mud-walled hut set in a tiny sun-dappled grove, he really looked like a lone ape. He had short stubby legs, grotesquely long, dangling arms, and a pleasant round face that seemed all the larger for the closely cropped hair. He loved to joke with his students and did dozens of flips and monkey imitations to entertain them.

The Monkey style employed acrobatics, *qinggong*, a loose body, concentrated mind, and external strength. Flexibility was paramount, and the Monkey master felt that relaxation was imperative not only to the physical and mental states necessary for monkey boxing, but for spirituality as well. He explained by using monkeys as an example.

"Look at all you Taoist boys," he giggled. "Someday you'll grow up to be priests with long lives of meditation. The monkeys have you beaten. They know meditation already.

"If you look quietly in the forests, you can come across a monkey sitting by a stream, just staring. He's not moving, he's not doing anything. He's just sitting. He's in complete stillness. Just think—he didn't need a Taoist to teach him.

"Or you might look up and see a monkey perched on a high tree top, completely lost in himself. He might be a hundred feet off the ground but he won't fall because he has complete, one-pointed concentration. Just look at you fellows. Why, you can hardly even stand properly!

"The monkey uses his mind while he is totally relaxed. He is unafraid because he knows his intelligence makes him superior. The monkey knows strategy, instinctively comprehending the saying, 'I move after the enemy, but arrive before him.' Attack a monkey. He'll roll away, take a watchful posture. He'll stay there for hours or days until your next move. You can't catch him off guard. The instant you move, he'll respond more quickly than you anticipate."

Strikes in the Monkey style were unique and varied, including double-knuckle punches, bitelike pinches, slaps, arcing fingers that caught eyes, nostrils, or lips, and devious overhead raps. Saihung also learned the unusual monkey stances, bow-legged off-center walks and jumps, because, as his teacher said, "A monkey cannot stand straight up so he is always moving. You must use this mobility in your fighting."

Sparring with the Monkey master was both hilarious and terrifying. In the beginning of each match he jumped absurdly around, mockingly allowing Saihung to strike him. He had the singular ability to take strikes anywhere on his body, including his kettlelike head. Saihung punched with abandon, and all the time the master bobbed ridiculously. Once the master decided to hit back, however, Saihung knew true terror and invariably ran away. But the teacher pursued him relentlessly, pounced on him with a monkey leap, showing Saihung that only the master was impervious to pain.

Saihung's fourth Wudangshan teacher was the Snake master, a cold, evil man. He did not want respect or warm regard from others. He only wanted to be feared, and all the other masters avoided him. A tall figure as flat and massive as a tombstone, staying ever in shadow, glaring unwelcomingly with reptilian intensity, and eating only cold food, the Snake master was a terrifying presence.

He trained in a yin power different from the Bat Immortal's metaphysical yin. His yin was darkness, dampness, and hell. He communed with the underworld without a care for his soul. Everything was secondary to power. He drew from the cold depths a devastating skill and merciless conviction that led him to total boxing superiority.

Out of all his teachers, Saihung genuinely feared only him. The Snake master was brutal during sparring, and when he broke his normal graveyard silence to speak, it was only to deliver a short, cutting remark. Ostensibly, he corrected his students, but in reality he always seized on their weakest personality flaws. Both he and his system were unrelentingly cruel.

The primary Snake strike was an open-handed strike with the fingertips. The Iron Luohan punched, the Crane pecked, and the Monkey pawed, but the Snake pierced. The Snake master wordlessly established his credentials with Saihung and the class by leading them to a butcher shop and repeatedly stabbing his hands through a side of beef.

"In order to have piercing strength," said the Snake master, "you must have internal energy that is as pliable as a blade of grass. A blade of grass gives with the wind. Even a hurricane cannot uproot it. It is so soft; yet it can cut your hand. It is this pliable energy you seek. No matter what your opponent hits you with, yield, slither, give way to his attack. Absorb his energy until the full extension of his strike, and then at that moment, when he is weakest, whip back ferociously."

His eyes glittered as he invited Saihung to attack. He evaded with a flexibility that made his body appear boneless. Saihung attempted grappling and locking, but the master's arms were like rubber. Then the Snake master lashed back with sadistic pleasure, his arms coiling around Saihung's head before a flurry of strikes left fingertip bruises all over Saihung's body.

"Your defenses are too open," announced the Snake master derisively. He noticed Saihung rubbing his sore spots. "If I don't hit you, you won't remember. This way, your body feels the pain and you'll never forget to guard your vulnerable points."

The ultimate strategy of the Snake system was to attack vital points. Strikes to these spots could cripple, damage internal organs, and even kill. Each day for a hundred days Saihung trained with fingertip pushups and hundreds of strikes to a hard sandbag. The Snake master insisted that the right effect could be achieved only if the fingers could be inserted into the opponent's body to a one-inch depth.

"A snake kills in several ways," said the master. "It bites, it chokes, and it hits vital spots. A snake catches an animal in its coils, and while the animal struggles the snake's tail hits the animal's vital spots. Our art is derived from watching this.

"The strike is not only physical, it is internal. The mind commands the energy into the fingertips as they hit your target. The precision is pinpointed." He struck Saihung lightly, and Saihung began to gasp desperately for air. The master let the class watch him struggle for several minutes before he released the effect by massage and a slap on the back.

"This is my system," he said. "It is dedicated to complete domination."

The Snake master was clearly psychopathic, but the Taoists kept him on Wudangshan so that he would be controlled and his art preserved by his teaching. The Grand Master continually emphasized this point to Saihung during his education with the martial artists: to learn and absorb a master's art is wise; to emulate his entire personality is foolish. Saihung endeavored to absorb all that Wudangshan had to offer and yet to maintain his own personal Taoist philosophy.

The great martial ability he acquired, combined with his

quick temper, made Saihung pugnacious. But his ever watchful Taoist teachers constantly reminded him to be humble. At the end of summer, he and his class left Wudangshan and were making their way back to Huashan, when they stopped at a teahouse. The priest escorting them summarized this Taoist viewpoint.

"Learning martial arts means self-assurance, not arrogance. Your confidence should make you the meekest, most humble person on earth. If you are secure in your techniques, nothing anyone can do has any meaning. It is impossible for them to annoy you because you know they cannot harm you. You know you can fight, but you do not exercise that ability. You remain free of violence.

"It is not the boxer who is dangerous, rather, it is the weakling. Insecure, the latter must constantly 'prove' himself. His weakness and ignorance make him arrogant."

"Hey, look at those Taoist boys!" cried out a man in the teahouse.

"Teenagers who have never known women!" laughed his companion.

Saihung's temper flared up instantly. The priest looked over at the men and smiled warmly.

"Walking away from a confrontation makes one superior," continued the priest to the class. "You have not been taught martial arts to kill, to win glory for yourself, nor to exalt religion. Rather, the purpose is self-discipline and self-defense."

"You mean they're all virgins?" shouted the man to his companion.

"I suppose," replied the other loudly. "In fact, maybe they don't even have any balls! Hey! Hey, little Taoists, do you have any balls?"

"Even if they do, I bet they're smaller than this peach pit!"

"Do you suppose they've ever seen a woman? Do they know what one looks like?"

"Hah! They probably wouldn't even know what to do with one!"

Saihung was ready to get up in a flash. His muscles tensed for a fight. He looked to the priest for a sign. The priest only turned lazily around to gaze kindly at the two laughing men.

Fixed by the priest's steady but nonaggressive stare, the two men gradually became quiet with embarrassment. When several minutes of silence had elapsed, the priest motioned the class to leave.

"Meeting people who demonstrate their ignorance is not an invitation to fight. Since you can remember your abilities, you can understand their plight. Rather than hate them, you should feel compassion."

FIFTEEN

Yang Chengfu and Taijiquan

WITH INTRODUCTIONS from his
master and grandfather, Saihung traveled frequently throughout the provinces and studied with such great boxers as Sun
Lutang and Bao Tianyi, of the Xingyi style, Fu Zhensong and
Zhang Zhaodong of the Bagua style, and Yang Chengfu of
Taiji style. The Grand Master wanted him to gain a good foundation in these internal martial arts, which stressed, in contrast to muscular external arts, the use of internal energy in
fighting, and the integral use of *qigong* and meditation in practice. Xingyi, Bagua, and Taiji were unique martial arts known
as moving meditations. Of these three arts, Taijiquan was the
highest form, and its greatest exponent was Yang Chengfu,
who taught at his own school in Beijing.

Saihung had known him from childhood, because Master
Yang had visited Huashan every summer. Saihung had always
called him "Uncle Yang," and the Taiji master affectionately
nicknamed him "Little Monkey." Now Little Monkey was in
his early teens, and he addressed the kindly Uncle as "Master."

Yang Chengfu welcomed Saihung warmly. He was a large
man, over six feet in height, and enormous. His shaved head
was like a bullet, and his compact face and heavy forehead
looked impervious to injury. Saihung knew that his old uncle
had two sides to his personality. One side he had heard of but
had not yet seen: Yang Chengfu was reputed to be a devastating and merciless fighter. The other side was refined and
scholarly, and it was this gentle, soft-spoken, bespectacled, and
almost bookwormish personality he knew who greeted Saihung.

Master Yang lived in a huge compound that was both home

to his family and a live-in school for those disciples giving themselves wholly to the study of Taijiquan. Saihung became, for a time, one of these students. As the grandson of a renowned martial artist and disciple of Huashan, he was accepted into the ranks of this select group.

In the following weeks, both senior disciples and the bespectacled Yang Chengfu introduced Saihung to Taijiquan. It was a complete system of therapeutic physical exercises, meditation, and martial art. In living up to its name, which meant the "Great Ultimate Fist," Taiji used a wide range of practices. Aside from its unusual, slow-moving set, Taiji had its own *qigong* set, standing and sitting meditations, a Taiji ruler (a piece of wood with two knobs on each end, a channel drilled through its center, and held between the two palms to direct internal energy from one hand to another), and the Taiji spheres (one being a three-foot-diameter stone sphere that was rolled around by the practitioner's leg, and a smaller sphere to develop the palms and fingers by rolling it on a concave table). All these techniques increased and trained internal energy until the practitioner could open his meridians and psychic centers.

With these practices, the Taiji set became a moving meditation that set into motion the microcosmic orbit, which vertically encircled the torso, and the macrocosmic orbit, a circuit through all four limbs. The internal energy traveling through these circuits naturally spilled into connecting meridians, powered the psychic centers, and massed potential human energy to tidal wave force. As a healing element, this flow of energy increased circulation, calmed the mind, relaxed the muscles, and healed nervous, organic, and skeletal problems. As a force for fighting, it's use allowed internal energy, not muscular force, to defeat the opponent. When a Taiji master stuck an enemy, his internal energy entered into the enemy's body, destroying body tissue more than a physical blow could ever do.

But the revolutionary nature of Taiji as a fighting art went beyond this. Taiji advocated relaxedness and lightness in contrast to other styles' principles of strength and heavy strikes. The Taiji practitioner remained relaxed and calm during a fight not simply for enhanced reflexes or clear thinking but also to allow his internal energy to flow unhindered by muscular tension. The relaxation then allowed the fighter to casually touch his opponent with enough sensitivity to detect the force and direction of incoming attacks. In turn, the softness of his own body yielded no clues to his own movement. This was the essence of deviousness in internal martial art.

Such sophisticated technique was fostered through Taiji Pushing Hands, an exercise where the students used circular movements of their touching hands to detect their partner's attack and thereby push him over, and through an extensive set of fighting techniques practiced as separate sparring routines. In fighting as well as healing, Taiji was indeed the Great Ultimate, and Yang Chengfu had to be constantly ready to prove it.

Saihung had the opportunity not only to see Taiji's technique but his Uncle Yang's reputed cruel side. One night the entire Yang family and school had gone out to dinner. As they left the restaurant, Yang Chengfu, walking at the head of the family, suddenly cried out, "Stand back!"

Two men dropped a "pig-catching-basket" on him. It was a narrow, coarsely woven, rattan cylinder that imprisoned his arms and body tightly. Master Yang struggled a bit, until one of the men gave him a kick and the basket rolled unrestrainedly down a hill.

The two assailants, probably men who sought fame through defeating the great Yang Chengfu, quickly followed with drawn sabers. Two accomplices waited at the bottom of the hill.

"Are you all here?" inquired Master Yang when he reached the bottom.

The men responded by raising their sabers.

"All right," said Master Yang. He inhaled mightily and flexed his arms. The basket ripped easily.

Master Yang stood up. By the dim glow of the street lanterns, he was suddenly a menacing juggernaut. "You wanted to take my life," he said in a low growl. "It's too bad you haven't made it. Take a look around. Today is your last day on earth."

The men attacked savagely. In an unhurried, methodical way, Yang Chengfu sidestepped the saber attacks and killed the first two men by dealing each a single blow over their hearts. He killed the last two in rapid succession, by snapping their necks. It was a casual matter to him.

In China's highly competitive martial world, no art could call itself the "Great Ultimate" unless it was prepared to prove it. Yang Chengfu's brother, father, uncle, and grandfather were all great fighters. Historically, Taijiquan established its standing in the martial world by successfully overcoming all challenges. Its only serious competition came from Xingyiquan and Baguazhang. In time, Xingyi, Bagua, and Taiji were integrated together to be known collectively as the "Internal System," with Taiji recognized as the highest form.

When Saihung was living in Master Yang's school, he noticed a bedridden man. Was this, he discreetly inquired of his classmates, a sick member of the Taiji school? No, they told him. It was a Xingyi master who had challenged Yang Chengfu four months ago and had lost. During the match the Xingyi master had attacked violently, and Yang Chengfu had initially contented himself with dodging. Before long, though, he wondered how seriously the Xingyi master intended to harm him. The Xingyi master was also an internal boxer and it was hard to decide. Just as his hand chopped at Yang Chengfu's head, Master Yang dodged, grabbed a vase, and held it where his own head had been. The Xingyi master could not check himself; his hand struck the vase. Nothing happened for several seconds; then the vase, which had remained whole, suddenly developed hairline cracks and disintegrated in Master Yang's hand. Seeing that the Xingyi master was truly using internal energy for the purpose of ultimate destruction, Yang Chengfu struck him with a single palm blow that sent his body crashing through the doors and left him bleeding from the eyes, nose, and mouth. It had not been a death blow, however, and Yang Chengfu kept the man in the school to heal him. The Xingyi master had not yet recovered, but everyone assured Saihung that he soon would.

Saihung would return to the school several times again to study Taiji, even after Master Yang's death. But before he left at the end of his first stay there, he saw Fu Zhensong, the Bagua master, challenge Yang Chengfu.

During the match Fu Zhensong, a short, stocky, and young fighter, circled Master Yang in the constant style of his Dragon Form Baguazhang. Yang Chengfu stood at the center of the circle in a standing meditative pose and closed his eyes. He was statically building up internal energy for the fight. Fu Zhensong, by circling, was dynamically charging himself up for the clash.

He circled for almost half an hour, never varying his pace. Master Yang remained still. Suddenly, Fu Zhensong dashed straight to the center. Master Yang's eyes opened instantly, and he knocked Fu Zhensong down. Following his opponent's stumbling body, he brought his fist and considerable body weight smashing down on Fu Zhensong's heart.

But Fu Zhensong also had great internal energy, so he was able to resist the force of the blow. Although he conceded defeat, he was able to walk away.

In this contest between internal systems, Saihung had been able to see the power of meditation, and the proven superiority of Taijiquan. He saw that Taiji was truly a great art form and sought to incorporate it into his boxing style. Taijiquan took twenty-five years to master fully. His short stay at Master Yang's school had been but an introduction.

SIXTEEN

The Grand Master
Challenges Saihung

Saihung, even before he had reached the age of fifteen, was a strong fighter. When his secular martial masters entered him in provincial tournaments he won his share of the matches. In his wanderings around the countryside, he was a dramatic figure, handsome, lean, and well-muscled. He had a wide, smooth-skinned face and braided hair that had been uncut since his first arrival on Huashan. He was a proud young man, brash and reckless in his challenges. At one time, he challenged two Praying Mantis teachers, and won only because he had concealed steel plates beneath his heavy clothing while boasting to the frustrated pair that it was his "internal energy" coming out. On another of his trips there was an even bolder challenge.

Passing through a town, Saihung had seen a notice in the village square announcing the arrival of the White Crane Society. The large sign had said, "White Crane: Under Heaven We Are the First" and "When We Are Here, There Is No Second Place."

Saihung had promptly written on the notice, "When I am here, you are second."

The next day, the White Crane Society left the note "If you dare, you'll be here tomorrow."

"I'll be here," wrote Saihung.

Five young men in the fanciest silk clothing were there the next day. Saihung appeared in his coarse gray Taoist robes.

"What? You? Why, you're just a kid," exclaimed the twenty-eight-year-old leader. "You are stupid for talking so big. Be-

Saihung at age sixteen

sides, I see you are a Taoist. I cannot fight a monk."

"I'm not a Taoist," responded Saihung. "I'm a wandering herbalist and martial artist."

"You kid! Even asleep I know more than you!"

"Hah! Only in your dreams do you know more than I!"

"Watch your mouth, kid!" roared the tall leader.

"How many will attack?" responded Saihung casually. "I'm only asking so I can tell the undertaker how many to expect."

"Don't talk so arrogantly. Only I need fight you. Tell me where you are from, little Taoist, so we know where to ship your stinking carcass!"

"That won't be necessary. Fight, if you are a man!"

The Crane boxer sprang forward. Saihung was still, gathering his qi. Just as the Crane boxer was almost on him, Saihung threw himself on the ground and brought a kick straight up into his opponent's groin. He hooked his other foot around the Crane boxer's ankle and tripped him.

Saihung jumped up and with his full weight crushed down on the man's abdomen. The he flipped the Crane boxer over and, spreading the boxer's legs into a frog's legs position, ripped the hip muscles.

"Didn't I tell you?" Saihung said mockingly as he strutted away. He felt completely triumphant and rejoiced in the superiority of his skills.

It was time for him to return to Huashan, yet he was reluctant. The pleasures of the world fascinated him. He enjoyed the wealth and prestige of his family; beautiful clothes; rich surroundings; and feasts of river fish, goose, and bear paws. He constantly savored his victories and began to yearn for the glories of a fighter. By comparison, the frugality of Huashan, its absolute discipline and life of extreme denial, seemed unbearable. But he was committed to return. Saihung began his ascent with a sigh.

The Grand Master summoned Saihung as soon as his disciple had returned to the mountain.

"You think you're pretty good, don't you?"

Saihung nodded confidently.

"You're not. You've been lucky. If you want to be good, you need meditation. Your internal system must be perfect. It is the internal that is the source of power, and you must go deep inside and use the totality of yourself in order to develop."

"I have won tournaments and challenges."

"You can be better if you meditate before your practice. It will unleash unusual energy."

"I already know internal martial arts. I can fight."

"But you do not go deep enough into meditation, and the spiritual, after all, is higher than fighting."

"Perhaps I'm not interested. It's great fun out there. I have, in my wanderings, been in the Peking Opera, joined a circus, and learned from many boxers. I would never have been able to do this if I had not been a wandering Taoist. Members of a holy order can't learn the most brutal parts of martial arts. I want to learn the ultimate in techniques, and I'd never be able to do that here on the mountain."

"You think your skill is so great?" asked the Grand Master casually.

"Yes, I do."

"Then fight me. If you win, I will introduce you to many masters. You'll be free to enter the outside martial world. But if you lose, you return to your studies. Agreed?"

Saihung looked at his master. Standing on a terrace overlooking a vast view of mountain ranges, they seemed alone at the top of the world. Saihung asked himself why he had climbed all that way simply to talk with this recluse who lived such a spare and severe life. Life seemed better down below, and in spite of years of training, the grand Master looked like any other old man. Saihung judged his master's weight. Saihung knew he outweighed him.

"I agree," said Saihung with a confident smile.

"All right," returned the Grand Master. "Fight!"

Saihung attacked immediately with strong and sure whirlwind strikes so swift that most men would have fallen simply because of their slower reflexes. The Grand Master, however, only retreated calmly before Saihung's advance. He let Saihung try all the boxing techniques gleaned from his many tournament bouts, but not even a single blow touched the Grand Master's robes.

Saihung grew angry, and gathering in his full might, charged his master. The Grand Master gracefully launched himself in a spinning leap over Saihung's shoulders. Saihung turned and struck out, but a whipping force sped by his face. A moment later, a devastating slap turned his head. It was the Grand Master's sleeve.

His master now took the initiative, and Saihung backed frantically away from his spinning arms. Through his blocks, he could see the Grand Master glaring ferociously at him as sleeve after sleeve came. Before long, his arms had been whipped numb. He dropped his guard. His master struck him with a palm blow, and Saihung flew across the terrace.

Saihung lay stunned on the stone pavement. The Grand Master came over to him. He was kind and smiling again. Helping Saihung up, he patted him reassuringly.

"You've lost," the Grand Master said softly. "You lost because you do not have enough concentration. I won because my concentration is complete. Concentration is impossible without meditation."

Saihung stood up and caught his breath.

"I'd still rather be a wandering Taoist. Look at you. Yes, you're a holy man. But what has it gotten you? You're starved. You live in damp rooms on a lonely mountaintop. You're a nobody. Are you successful? Do the gods listen to you? Will you go to heaven? How do you know there's even such a thing as heaven?"

"You can only see the gods and heaven by mastering this world," replied the Grand Master patiently. "Then you can see the next world.

"I admit that if I were to see heaven, I might believe, but

how can I go to heaven? Wouldn't I fall out of the sky?

"Not the body," laughed the Grand Master. "Your spirit travels to heaven and returns. That is the way."

"Your spirit? Can it come out from the body?"

"Oh yes. But you must control the senses. When you realize that this world is an illusion, you can control the senses, master the world, and travel on."

"The world is an illusion?"

"Yes. Nothing is real."

"What do you mean, 'Nothing is real'? Of course this world is real!"

"It isn't. It's illusion. Once you master your senses and the Five Elements, you will know that, too."

"I don't believe you. How do I know what 'mastering the senses' and 'mastering the world' mean?"

The Grand Master looked at Saihung placidly. "This, Saihung, is mastery of the world." He pointed dramatically across the terrace at an unlit stick of incense. It lit immediately. Sandalwood fragrance drifted toward them.

"And it is also this," said the Grand Master.

He pointed at a heavy brass teapot on a table six feet away. It floated up and moved slowly in the air to another table. Saihung was dumbfounded.

"Master the Five Elements and then you can see the other world. But you have to study if you want to achieve this. Contemplate this. Make a decision. Some things must be begun in youth to achieve success later. A tree grows from a seed. I know it's difficult for you to believe. You're young. You haven't seen fruit. That's why I show you. But you cannot always demand complete proof before you begin something. In some things you must have blind faith. The gods are supreme. They will let you know."

SEVENTEEN

The Second and Third Pillars

 M EDITATION IS not simply
something you do by itself, casually," said the Grand Master.
"Other disciplines complement it and must also be mastered.
Martial arts generate mighty strength, and the raw energy for
meditation, but the mind must be cultivated through music,
calligraphy, painting, and metaphysics before you can be
ready for contemplation.

"Music is the direct link between the soul and the divine.
The body is like a hollow reed, and music fills it with the song
of the gods. Music will calm you, sooth your nerves, tell you
of otherworldliness. Even in the midst of great turmoil music
can bring peace to your heart. No one lives without music.
You must learn to play music, to experience not only the
sounds but to accept its physical benefits as well. Playing the
flute, for example, trains the mind and qi to act in unison and
stimulates the meridians in the fingertips. Whether you listen
or whether you play, music refines your soul. It is peace, emotion, expression, and the sound of the sacred.

"Calligraphy is calming and unifying. The brush is an extension of the hand and moving it stimulates the meridians,
moves the skeletal system, soothes the nerves, relaxes the
mind, and develops the ability to absorb poetry. By copying
poetry, you ponder the nuances and subtleties unnoticeable in
reading. The original intent of the poets and sages are absorbed by tracing their exact strokes. Viewing and copying calligraphy will tell you what the scriptures mean. The actual act
of calligraphy makes you calm, gentle, rational, and intelligent.

"Painting also has this dual purpose: it can be an expression
of an artist's inner working, but it can also be a method of

taking the outside world directly into the psyche. As expression, art is the exercise of beauty. It comes from the heart, not the mind, stimulates compassion and joy, and nourishes the beauty of your inner soul.

"Beauty implies appreciation. The painter expresses his appreciation of nature's beauty but he also absorbs natural beauty through painting. What the eye sees goes directly into the soul. In this regard, spiritual diagrams are also painting, and can lead one to the divine. Thus, both in presenting nature and other art, painting directly affects the personality."

Saihung was assigned classes in music, calligraphy, and painting in addition to a heavy curriculum of philosophy, anthropology, archeology, astronomy, meteorology, and the classics. All his courses were designed to expand his mind, discipline him, and refine his temperament. The Grand Master also gave instruction on the metaphysical arts of talismanic writing, the summoning of spirits, and divination. Added to the pillar of his physical training, the arts and metaphysics were the second and third pillars; these three areas together were the foundations for meditation.

Divination familiarized Saihung with Taoist cosmology and provided him with a way of receiving the words of the gods. The Grand Master understood Saihung's reluctance to believe in something unseen and unheard. The Taoist answer was to communicate directly to the spirits and gods through visualization and divination in order to prove their existence. The *I Ching*, a holy book characterizing the universal cosmological principle as change through the interaction of yin and yang and the transmutations of the *Ba Gua*, was based on sixty-four hexagrams that embodied all cosmic states. The *I Ching* itself was a codification of an even earlier system of divination devised by Fu Xi. This legendary sage who lived over 5,000 years ago, represented the polar forces of the world, yin and yang, by either a broken line or an unbroken one. While in a trance, he happened to glimpse a turtle shell and in that moment formulated the *Ba Gua*, an octagonal arrangement of the trigrams that represented the eight possible triple combinations of broken and unbroken lines. Each trigram represented different natural forces: heaven, earth, thunder, water, mountain, wood, fire, and lake. From its very premise, Taoist divination was a perception of the movement and circumstance created by natural forces.

The eight trigrams were later combined into all their possible combinations, resulting in the sixty-four hexagrams that formed the basis of the *I Ching*. This was done by King Wan while he was held captive in prison during the twelfth century. He named each hexagram and wrote a commentary on each one. After his death, his son, the Duke of Zhou, added commentaries to each individual line of each hexagram. The work of both men formed the inner structure to the *I Ching*, a structure that in successive centuries was augmented by numerous scholars, including Confucius himself.

But to simply expose Saihung to such a difficult and ancient holy book was something the Grand Master was too wise to do. He wanted Saihung to understand divination and the philosophy of the *I Ching* more directly, so he took him to see the Ancient Oracle.

As they had in years before, master and student trekked together into the remote mountains. During the journey, the Grand Master told Saihung the story of the Oracle.

"Five hundred years ago, the Taoists of Huashan chanced on a man nearly dead of exposure. No one knew where he had come from and the man revealed nothing of his past and pointedly disavowed any connection with Taoism. He was too weak to be moved. They nursed him back to health on that mountaintop.

"He recovered and simply announced that he would stay on that spot to 'practice his art.' What that art might be was a mystery even to the oldest Taoists. The man sat down at the foot of a large cypress tree on the edge of a high ledge. He never moved again.

"The Taoists supplied him with food and water but the man

Yin   Yang

Greater Yin   Lesser Yin   Lesser Yang   Greater Yang

Earth   Mountain   Water   Wood   Thunder   Fire   Lake   Heaven

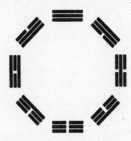

The *Ba Gua:* eight trigrams arranged in a circle

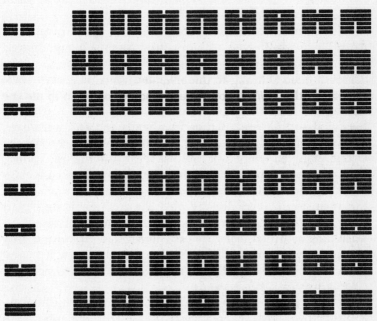

The sixty-four hexagrams of the I Ching *as they are
derived from the eight trigrams*

Derivation of the sixty-four hexagrams from Yin and Yang

stopped eating entirely. His hair grew directly into the tree and he gained all his nourishment from that.

"'Never cut my hair, it is my lifeblood,' he said. But one day, a curious young acolyte crept up from behind and cut several strands, whereupon the man froze the intruder with magic. The man became severely ill and the tree withered.

"'So, you tried to take my life. I'll take yours instead,' said the Oracle. He transformed the boy into a tree, and over the centuries, his hair continued to grow until it pierced into the trunk which was the transformed boy. They say it's still the boy who stands there, sheltering the Ancient Oracle.

"The Oracle has memorized the entire *I Ching*, and can attain the applicable hexagram not by tools, but by going into a trance and receiving the hexagram directly from the spirit of Fu Xi, the originator of *Ba Gua*."

Saihung and his master made their way up an overgrown path. There was indeed a figure sitting against a cypress tree. They prostrated themselves before him.

Saihung looked up at the wizened man. His eyes were closed, his skin dry, his beard scraggly and uncut. Someone had draped leopard skins on his shoulders and lap, covering his faded and tattered clothes. His hands and feet were bare, the long nails curling. Saihung noticed incredulously that the Oracle's tangled white hair did disappear into the tree trunk.

The Ancient Oracle opened his eyes. Saihung asked a question. The Oracle closed his eyes for a minute and then, opening them again, verbally revealed the hexagrams and their changes. From their formations, he interpreted an answer.

Saihung returned many times. The Ancient Oracle not only knew in advance of Saihung's coming, but also knew his questions. Whenever Saihung went to him, the Ancient Oracle had already prepared his answer.

Eventually, Saihung learned to use the *I Ching* by himself, and this gave him a pragmatic experience with the application of Taoist philosophy in everyday life. The *I Ching* gave its answer after Saihung constructed a hexagram from coin tosses.

He put three coins into a turtle shell; these were Fu Xi's original tools of divination. He shook the shell until the coins fell out. Depending on the pattern into which the coins fell, a certain line was implied. It could be Yin, Yang, Changing Yin, or Changing Yang. From six tosses, the hexagram could be constructed. Saihung would consult the *I Ching* about that hexagram, and if it had changing lines he would also look up the hexagram made by the change. Change was the central theme of the *I Ching*, and how life changed was its most important lesson. Through his study and practice, Saihung learned the wisdom of *I Ching*: that change was natural, that yielding and action were both important, that there were certain personal requirements the gods demanded if ill consequences were to be avoided, and that whenever an event reached its zenith, it automatically began to change to its opposite.

The Grand Master finally introduced elementary meditation to Saihung. As in all his training, the learning proceeded from the simple to the complex in cumulative stages strictly controlled by the Grand Master. Nothing was to be left to chance. The Grand Master explained the procedure to him and warned him in advance of what he would experience. There was always a task to be achieved in his meditations, and Saihung was required to report all that happened to him in the process. The Grand Master then either confirmed the validity of Saihung's experience or rejected it as hallucination.

"In our tradition," said the Grand Master, "meditation is impossible without a pure body, open meridians, and *qi*. We've explained to you since childhood: without *qi*, there is no spirit. We require also that the trainee have a refined personality. Otherwise, a monster could emerge. Finally, the trainee must know something of cosmology, which provides the right context.

"You begin meditation upon these foundations. There are three kinds of meditation: moving, standing, and sitting. You have already experienced moving meditation by learning

Xingyi, Bagua, Taiji, and the Five Animals. In moving meditation, the external is dynamic, but the internal is still. In standing meditation, the external is static, but the inside moves. This is where you shall begin."

Standing meditation was a series of static postures combined with specific hand gestures. Saihung was taught to use them to stimulate certain organs, excite the flow of energy to the meridians, and strengthen the body. Although the body position was a factor, the crucial force was the mind. Standing meditation developed concentration with pinpoint accuracy.

This ability to concentrate was further consolidated by visualization and *kow hou*, or invocation. One set of standing meditations built the three *dan tians* at the navel, solar plexus, and eyebrow. Saihung concentrated individually on each one, simultaneously visualizing from pictures the god of that *dan tian*, invoking the god's name repeatedly, and directing his breath to that area. There was no opportunity for his mind to wander if he was to complete the task. Confirmation came during the meditation: his body grew hot and his palms turned red.

At the end of his meditations, Saihung performed a series of dispersals. This was a hallmark Taoist procedure that dispersed the energy accumulated during meditation. The Taoists felt that meditation concentrated blood and *qi* in various centers, but primarily in the brain. Unless the accumulation was released and the entire body made neutral again, headaches, loss of hair, nervousness, insanity, heart problems, and hemorrhaging could result.

This philosophy completed the explanation of meditation. Meditation was an activity to be undertaken only after long years of preparation and the attainment of perfect health. It unleashed great forces in the body and accelerated the circulation. Unless a body had been strengthened, it could not withstand the shock. Sometimes breathing slowed so much that it stopped spontaneously. Without *qigong* training, the practitioner would pass out.

"Now you see how you've changed," said the Grand Master, a year after he had "challenged" Saihung. "You see that meditation is supported by the three pillars of your previous training. You find yourself of a calmer temperament, and you believe it because it works. It gives you measurable results. Now you have an inkling of what it is to be an internalist. Nothing in the outside world compares. It is the basis of your life, and you must go deeper and deeper."

PART FOUR

RENUNCIATION

EIGHTEEN

A Decision Made Alone

S<small>AIHUNG'S SUCCESS</small> in his practices brought on a period of self-evaluation. He had come to the point where, as an ordinary adept, he would automatically have taken vows of renunciation. But Saihung was not an ordinary adept. He had received special consideration and had been allowed to travel regularly. Guan Jiuyin had viewed Saihung's education on Huashan as a special one, but had expected that Saihung would return to the outside world, and the Grand Master's primary concern was to raise this difficult boy and educate him to the standards of his clan. Now the course had come to a culmination. Saihung had to make a decision: return to society or enter fully into Taoist asceticism.

In China, a sixteen-year-old was already an adult. Saihung was to decide alone. He trusted only his grandfather and master, but neither one wanted to influence him. He was free to do as he wished.

The Grand Master bade him go down from the mountain and return to his family for deliberation. As Saihung left the mountain, he suddenly felt that the Taoists of Huashan remained as mysterious and unfathomable as when he had first met them. The Taoists were ascetics. Ascetics were not in need of anything from society, and life and death were the same to them. That unique independence from everything that normal people craved or feared was both appealing and frightening. Saihung had followed twin paths throughout his upbringing. He knew the ascetic path and the worldly one of his family and martial society, and although he had never before considered the implications of his anomalous situation, he now had to choose his future.

Saihung walked into the countryside of Shaanxi. He was an

unusual figure, exuding the pure physicality and inner confidence of his training. It was uncommon to see such a healthy youth on the poverty- and war-stricken plains, and many of the travelers could barely keep themselves from gawking.

It was in the 1930s, the province had seen great strife and had never recovered from the recent Communist and Kuomintang battles in her northern section. The land was ruined; the populace was starving. Saihung had seen the devastation in his previous travels, and had felt as helpless as the rest of the people. With the necessity of his imminent decision, he was careful to observe everything and eager to learn the latest news. He constantly asked himself if he wanted to be a part of this world.

He crossed the plains of Shaanxi, the land where much of Chinese civilization began. Centuries of history sprawled outward from the silk road that ended at Xian, like flower blossoms at the end of a long stem. It was an area that had seen culture, politics, warfare, and natural calamities come and go as regularly and inexorably as the flooding of the Yellow River.

What he saw and felt over the following days became a convolution of experiences without the perspective and artificial organization of second-hand history. Because he deliberately absorbed everything, the insane paradoxes of Chinese society, its extremes of wisdom and ignorance, wealth and poverty, benevolence and slavery, abundance and famine, power and helplessness, branded themselves into his mind.

He constantly tried to imagine his fate if he were to reenter society, and naturally began by trying to compare himself with other men his age. There weren't many among the peasants. Famine and conscription had decimated the population. Many of those left had joined such illicit warlord-sanctioned activities as pimping, gambling, and slave dealing.

The peasants' life was one of desperation. They were simultaneously ennobled by their attempt to wrest a meager yield from the parched land, and degraded by their exploitation.

The peasants depended on their ancestral lands, but they tilled overworked earth. Their mud homes were falling apart. Many buildings had been wrecked by soldiers who took doors on which to sleep and framing for fuel. The weather did the rest to destroy the small rooms into which families crowded as chaos increased. Snakes, lizards, and roaches crawled through at will. Rats, desperate for food, regularly attacked unattended infants. Pigs and farm animals, brought inside to prevent theft, left their filth everywhere. Disease was rampant. It was surprising that as many people as there were survived, to repeat the next day the wretched experiences of the days past.

Communist and Nationalist agents regularly tried to recruit reinforcements from a population desperate for relief. The Communists appealed to anti-Japanese sentiment and expressed ideals of agrarian reform. The Nationalists voiced anti-communist sentiments and praised the glories of the existing central government. Only the young listened to them. The old had heard too many promises already.

In some ways, the Communists were preferable to the Nationalists. Although they were repetitive in propagandizing their idealistic programs they did not, like Nationalists, shoot opponents in wholesale lots. But when soldiers came instead of cadres, Saihung saw little difference. Soldiers, whether Communist, Nationalist, or warlord, caused universal suffering. Seizing homes, food, and supplies; trampling crops, garrisoning in temples, using shrines for stables, raping, looting, torturing, and killing—not just the enemy but anyone they wished—were all commonplace practices. The cruelty inflicted on the people simply for the perverted enjoyment of the soldiers occurred with such monotonous regularity that the survivors took horror for granted.

Many tried to adapt, like organisms adapting to some new environment, becoming opportunists so far from human that Saihung could barely contain his revulsion. Some people sold their babies for slaves. Others sold human flesh and hearts as pork. Every sort of ugliness and villainy was in plain view.

Cheating merchants, dishonest officials, unrestrained soldiers, overzealous white missionaries, European slave traders—all preyed regularly on the rotting society. Even "paragons" of virtue and justice turned to exploiting the population.

Saihung saw that scholars and aristocrats, people who had appeared formerly as examples of righteousness, were now the most hypocritical and despicable of all. Insensitive to the miseries of the villagers, they strolled about in fine silken clothing, casually fluttering their exquisite fans. Purposefully conspicuous on streets lined with beggars and the lower class, they almost seemed to welcome the suffering. In their shortsighted way, Saihung thought, they enjoyed this state of affairs, because it highlighted their status and gave them continuing opportunities to exact profits. They were self-centered and repressive. Nothing seemed to matter as long as they could continue to stand on the backs of the peasantry.

As Saihung journeyed on toward his home, the sight of a predatory society feeding on its self became overpowering. He was a participant in a mad carnival. It was a walk with death never out of sight. A parade with dogs and crows presiding over corpses. A march of girls sold into prostitution, or coerced into arranged marriages. A line of pathetic human caricatures with open sores, bulging tumors, severed limbs, tubercular wheezes, hunchbacks, and mutilated faces. Saihung gave away what money he had, but it was miniscule in proportion to the overwhelmingly grotesque needs. He remained a helpless walker, a part of the procession of terror, until he reached his ancestral home.

The heavy gates closed behind him, and the family and servants received him enthusiastically. With great fanfare, he was welcomed back into the Guan family mansion. Saihung felt the familiarity and security of his childhood home. The beautiful architecture, serene gardens, and the high walls were all intact. But as he walked beneath wisteria-laced archways, over hand-carved foot bridges, and past trees planted by his ancestors four generations ago, he wondered whether it was he or the world that had changed. He tried to reconcile the turmoil through which he had traveled and the paradise of the mansion. Had the contrasts existed before? Had he simply been unaware?

He reflected that he had never really taken a long-range view of his life. He had allowed his master and grandfather to set a course for him and had followed it. But now he saw himself torn between extremes—between wealth and poverty, between duty and want, between renunciation and worldliness. He had closed his mind to all social problems, when immersed either in his training or in the diversions his family status provided. On Huashan, he knew the thrill of new knowledge; while at home, he could claim his legacy of fine clothes, purebred horses, delicious feasts, attentive servants, art collections, and rare weapons. Until now, he had ignored the contradictions of his unusual upbringing, the demands of his parents, and the responsibilities of his clan. He had, in fact, deferred all responsibility.

He sat down before the pond and gazebo where he had spent so many evenings with his grandparents. No memories, precedents, nor inspirations came to him. He had to find his own way. After he examined thoroughly his possible alternatives, Saihung decided he would leave the Guan family mansion.

He knew that his grandparents would continue to support him spiritually and financially. He admired both of them, but he also knew that their time was declining. Saihung was also sure his parents would oppose him, but dismissed them because he resented their standards. As for his uncles and aunts, he was tired of their petty squabblings and devious intraclan intrigues and had no qualms in walking away from them. Saihung braced himself for the furor his decision would create. Although he was certain that his grandparents would eventually accept his choice, he already felt the disapproval of all the others in his collective clan.

Renunciation and entering a religious order was a disgrace to a Chinese family. The Chinese words for a renunciate literally meant "one-who-has-left-one's-family," and to do this in a Confucian society, with its heavy emphasis on filial piety, was a sin. When one renounced, one became a nonperson. The family would act as if the renunciate had never existed. One's name, place in the clan records, representation in the family temple—every possible trace of one's identity was expunged. The family completely disavowed him because there would be no one in his place to carry on the clan, beget heirs, or increase its wealth and status.

Saihung went to see his grandfather, entering the library where he had first met the two acolytes. He quietly announced his decision.

Guan Jiuyin sat back in his chair and thoughtfully stroked his beard. He looked at his grandson for a long time before articulating carefully chosen words.

"I sent you up to the mountain to learn, build your strength, and be disciplined, acquire an unbreakable principle and will. But I expected that you would thereafter return to the clan."

Saihung was silent. He thought of his many classmates who, having graduated from Huashan, had indeed returned to secular life to become scholars, artists, martial heroes, or simply eccentric wanderers. Each was without a doubt a singular man, but few had disavowed all worldly attachments. Out of all the thousands educated on the mountain, few chose, or were eligible to become ascetics. Saihung vacillated.

"You are a member of a great clan," continued his grandfather. "Wealth, prestige, and power are your birthright; one might even say, duty. You can enjoy it. When you are here, you have no trouble. Do you truly want to walk away from it all?"

Saihung felt the glory of the mansion, that enormous dragon sprawling on the hillside. He considered again. But instead of regret, he only felt a curious dullness, an aloof elation. Saihung looked down and finally replied, "Yes."

Guan Jiuyin sighed and gave his approval.

The news of Saihung's decision went through the mansion swiftly. Even though Saihung tried to spend as much time as possible alone in the gardens, he was acutely aware of the disapproving stares.

He could not avoid a confrontation with his parents, however, and they clashed with him every day. Although they realized the futility of arguing, since the clan patriarch supported Saihung, they nevertheless protested his decision—the mother arguing because Saihung would not be a scholar, the father angry because Saihung would not be a soldier. They argued even on the day of his departure.

"You don't care about me as a person," Saihung finally said. "You only want me to succeed because it would bring prestige to you and the clan."

"That is your duty as a person," retorted his mother. "Have you, in your unfilial thinking, forgotten what duty is? You have to be a productive member of society and live up to the family name. Think of the responsibilities you are neglecting."

"Yes, think about it!" broke in his father emotionally. "Instead of meeting your obligations, you want to run off and become a wretched priest! What's so good about following some old, skinny, fairytale man around barren mountains? What does a damn priest do but sit around all day pretending that he's mumbling to the sages? All those fellows are deluded. They're bums, burdens on society, beggars who don't work. Carrying on their ostensible spirituality depends on the goodwill of others. Priests make their living skimming off the top of society's labors."

"Entering religious life disgraces the family," said his mother. "You should think of returning to your family if only because of the debt you owe them for raising you from a miserable child."

Saihung jumped up. His parents watched him from where they sat stiffly and formally. Saihung tried to voice his feelings, but he had no clever retorts, no simple irrefutable explanation. He felt pressure build in his head until he burst out with a heated farewell.

"Look, I only came to say goodbye. If I were uncaring, like you two, or like my brothers, I wouldn't even have returned to say anything. I would have just taken my vows and let all you worldly opportunists go to hell! Instead, I came back. Doesn't that show I am doing my last duty as a son? My mind is made up. I'm leaving!"

He broke from the room to curses from his angry father. A wave of panic swelled within him. He wanted to leave the mansion immediately. But he was still in the prison of obligations. He had still another gate through which he must pass: he had to talk to his betrothed.

When he was five years old, Saihung had been engaged to a girl two years older than he. The girl had then been taken into the Guan family at the age of nine to be reared and nurtured by the family of her future in-laws. This was an accepted custom to ensure complete compatibility with her future husband's family. She was already weeping when Saihung came to say goodbye.

"I'm going to be an old spinster if you abandon me," she sobbed.

Saihung looked at her. Dressed in her finest gown, her hair perfectly combed and pinned with flowers, she sat in the beautiful reception room of his home. He could see that her entire world extended no further than the women's chambers. She was the daughter of an extremely powerful general, and the marriage had been arranged to tie the two families together. He knew that all she wanted was to be his wife. That had been her sole upbringing.

"I'm already eighteen," she pleaded. "No man will want me now. I may even lose the protection of your family."

"I'm sorry," said Saihung. "You can always marry another man."

"I'm too old. I've been betrothed to you. How can you break our engagement so cruelly?"

Saihung tried to answer. His desperation to leave churned inside him. He tried to think. If his life had gone normally, he would already have married, at the age of fifteen, a girl he did not even know. He attempted another explanation, but she only wept more.

How to cope with a crying girl had simply not been covered in Saihung's extensive education. While he felt sympathy, he also felt the urgent need to leave. He asked her to stop crying, but she couldn't. Finally, his helplessness overcame him.

"I've never touched you!" he said roughly. "You're free to marry anyone else. I hope you can find happiness with him!"

He bolted from the room, slamming the inlaid lattice doors, hoping he could close out her hysterical cries. It was too much for him. Saihung went immediately to get his belongings.

He fled the mansion to curses, mockery, and accusations of betrayal from his entire clan. No one came forth to congratulate him or express support. He walked through the heavy datewood gates. As soon as they shut, he was alone with his doubt.

NINETEEN

Initiation

SAIHUNG KNELT down in the main hall of the South Peak Temple, the Hall of the Three Pure Ones (the Taoist trinity of Lao Tzu, the Jade Emperor, and the Original Being). It was a large, high-ceilinged, ornately decorated room sparkling with hundreds of slender burning tapers. Plain wood pillars supported partly gilded and partly painted carved archways depicting scenes of the Monkey King in Heaven and his exploits in fighting demons. At the head of the hall was an intricately carved, ceiling-high façade behind which were hung scrolls showing the Three Pure Ones, surrounded by hundreds of other gods. They had all been painted to look directly at the viewer, and the perspective gave them the appearance of floating off the picture plane. It was a grand, overwhelming vision of the heavenly host descending toward a single point, and Saihung knelt at that exact place.

The heavy rosewood altar table was set with all the necessary offerings, but it had several ritual objects different from normal altars. A gourd, symbol of renunciation; a horse-tail whisk, emblem of a Taoist master; and a comb for the ceremony, were special implements.

Other scrolls were hung on the side walls. Some were of calligraphy, others portraits of past ascetics and grand masters, and some depicted members of the Taoist pantheon. Together with those of the Three Pure Ones, the Jade Emperor, the Eight Immortals, Guan Yin (Kuan Yin), the Seven Princesses, and the Taoist hell, all the gods in the universe were present in witness.

As he awaited his initiation, doubt still consumed Saihung. But all the members of the South Peak Temple, the Grand Master, the two acolytes, and his grandparents were all in attendance. Every time he panicked, he looked around at them. They had been with him constantly from the beginning. Saihung trusted them and hoped that faith would carry him through.

The elders were solemn and sat stoically. It was a momentous occasion but their seriousness also seemed to include an awareness of Saihung's conflicting feelings. Only the two acolytes, still youths themselves, showed expressions of kindness and compassion. They smiled and gave him surreptitious looks of encouragement during the ceremony. These two were sympathetic; they knew his inner conflict.

The ceremony began. The assembly joined the Grand Master in a responsive recitation of the scriptures, punctuated by strikes on the bell, the gong, and the wooden fish. The smoke of the incense filled the hall, and the undulating flames from the oil lamps and candles gave a golden glow to the room. A hazy, otherworldly feeling came over Saihung as he recited alone.

He bowed nine times to the altar while offering incense, bowed to the past grand masters, and bowed nine times to his own Grand Master. He then made offerings of food, tea, and wine.

The Grand Master walked behind Saihung and combed his long black hair. This represented the combing away of all his past *ming huan,* all the consequences and attachments of his past lives. The Grand Master continued to recite and put Saihung's hair into a coil on his head and then pegged it expertly with a wooden hairpin. Saihung had now left his family.

The Grand Master taught Saihung his personal Taoist name and verse. These words were taken from the *Thousand Word Text.* According to the sequence of characters, Saihung's name identified him immediately to other Taoists. The verse was a code that authenticated his membership, generation, rank within his sect, and rank of the sect itself.

The two acolytes presented Saihung with neatly folded gray robes, cotton shoes, and prayer mat, copper begging bowl, and a special sutra for the next twelve years of his training. There was more recitation before Saihung went alone to worship in five separate shrines honoring the gods, immortals, and ascetics particularly related to his school. Afterward, he rejoined the assembly for a huge vegetarian feast.

He was committed, but privately he still harbored doubts and fears. Uncertainty and insecurity made him wonder if he had irrevocably chosen an unhappy path. But he had seen China and he had known his family home—neither held any appeal for him. Saihung knew that this was his only real choice.

TWENTY

Internal Alchemy

As an initiated Taoist adept, Saihung began training in the esoteric practices of his sect. His practices of internal alchemy, including hygiene, therapeutic movement, and meditation would lead to a very special culmination.

Hygiene reflected the Taoist desire to purify the body, cleansing it of toxins that inhibited spiritual growth. In spite of their meticulously scrupulous diets and *qigong* exercises, the Taoists still felt that the body accumulated poisons.

"Every day while you breathe," stated his master, "your body collects dust, dirt, and other particles from the air. When you sleep, those substances remain in your lungs and enter your bloodstream. In addition, your body itself creates waste gases. All these things must be purged daily."

The Grand Master instructed Saihung in even more vigorous *qigong* exercises, and introduced special herbs to flush out his system. An herbal tea made up of five different flowers cleansed his digestive tract, another of roots and leaves cleansed his blood. Other formulas dissolved clotted blood, dispersed trapped *qi*, or relieved unbalanced organs.

Purification was followed by tonification, using ginseng and other herbs. These were even more powerful than the herbs Saihung had received during his Luohan training and were intended not only to maintain or strengthen the body, but to alter it permanently. This use of herbs and the accompanying training in meditation were integral to the sect's practice of internal alchemy.

Transformation of the human body was a deep-rooted Taoist tradition that was directed toward achieving immortality. Different sects had varying methods. Some insisted on complete abstention from meat, breads, and grains, and said that immortality could be gained by ingesting smelted gold, cinnabar, mercury, lead, and a variety of other metals. Others, such as Wang Je, the legendary twelfth-century founder of the Northern School, fanatically demanded the avoidance of all things that pleased the senses, abstinence from sleep, and the practice of total meditation in order to replace mortal breath with divine breath. Still others insisted that immortality came through the development of an immortal embryo in the *dan tian*, and some finally said that it was all symbolic: lead was yang, mercury was yin, and the embryo was not physical but was the enlightenment gained from returning to one's original spirit.

But no matter what the sect, internal alchemy always ranged between meditation and chemistry. Many died in their attempts, and the Taoists asserted that those who succeeded became immortal and ascended to heaven, thereby becoming unavailable as evidence. The only way to choose from the plethora of methodologies was by the guidance of a master. The Grand Master, who instructed Saihung, advocated nothing fanatical. He asserted that the chemicals were herbs, the smelting process took place in the cauldron of one's *dan tian*, and that the final alchemical transformation came through meditation.

"There is no such thing as immortality in its true sense," stated the Grand Master. "Immortality means longevity. Through correct practices, you can prolong your life to an unusual limit and remain free from illness. But no one lives forever. Even the gods must die.

"We can only taste immortality, but the practices can never be interrupted. Never neglect your body. If you train your mind but ignore your body, it will atrophy. If you neglect your mind and train your body, you'll never advance. The secret is that mind and body are united and that one can combine their energy to transcend this mortal plane."

Saihung's practice of internal alchemy took place in a small hut set aside solely for meditators. He was to stay there for forty-nine days to achieve the goal of opening his meridians in a process known as the "microcosmic orbit." The hut was a tiny mud-walled structure with a tile roof, a single shuttered window, and a "Dutch" door. Its only furnishings were a bed, a candlestick, and a low, square bench. When the Grand Master led Saihung inside, Saihung wondered if he would feel claustrophobic. The room was so small that he could have touched all four walls without moving from the center.

Saihung placed a woven grass mat on the bench. Over that he laid down a deerskin, followed by his own prayer rug. The grass mat was an insulator, the animal skin contributed the psychic energy of the deer, and the prayer rug was his own meditation aid. Saihung was to sit there for several hours every day of the forty-nine.

The Grand Master showed Saihung the proper seated posture. Saihung sat on the edge of the bench with his feet resting on the floor. He relaxed completely, keeping his spine perfectly straight, head raised with chin tucked in, and hands clasped in a special prayer gesture.

The Grand Master offered incense, explaining that it placated the senses and enhanced concentration. But Saihung had always found it distracting. He refused it.

He looked at the special manuals and books his master supplied. They gave directions and diagrams to help him achieve his breakthrough. In particular, Saihung was working on the two meridians on the center line of his body and he had to have a detailed knowledge of anatomy, meridians, and meridian points. The Grand Master explained each diagram, gave oral instructions, and waited while Saihung attempted the meditation for the first time. When he had completed it, he recounted his experiences and the Grand Master affirmed that his sensations indicated that he was practicing correctly.

Then the Grand Master left Saihung. Closing the door, he pasted a paper strip over the bottom edge of the door's lower half. The seal was both a talisman to drive away evil spirits and to prevent either Saihung from leaving or anyone from entering. Saihung could open only the top half for sunlight and for food and waste to be passed back and forth.

The microcosmic orbit was an attempt to join the two center-line meridians and mentally direct the flow of energy so that it would complete one revolution during a single cycle of inhalation and exhalation. Completing the circuit would enable him to send the energy further into his twelve meridians and eight psychic channels. If he succeeded, his body would be purified, body ailments would be healed, and he could learn to transmute the energy further into spirit and then stillness.

The meditation began at the navel. Saihung concentrated on that spot with patterns of visualization and incantations. After half an hour, he felt a buzzing vibration at his navel. It grew warm, and began to pulsate violently. He tried to send it downward to the next spot at the perineum. It was difficult, and he concentrated fully. The meridian opened in a painful line.

He was relieved that his initial attempt had been successful. Some other practitioners had such deep meridians or such little inclination for meditation that their masters resorted to herbs, massage, acupuncture, or even a jolt of energy from the master's own body to stimulate the flow of energy.

Over the forty-nine days, Saihung continued to extend his progress. Segment by segment he pushed the heated line from the tailbone to the point between the kidneys, to the point between the shoulderblades, to the base of the head, the crown, and finally to its terminus at the upper lip. By pressing his tongue to his upper palate, he connected the back meridian with the front and completed the circuit by opening up the final channel to connect back to the navel. The circuit was a continuing rush of heat, electricity, whirling sensations at the junction points, and a rhythmic tugging feeling on his spine. Taoist meditation resulted in these real confirmatory sensations, and Saihung was happy that he had succeeded in the complete procedure.

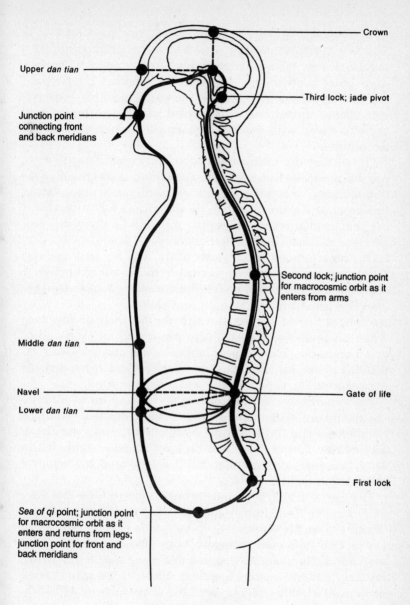

Crown

Upper *dan tian*

Third lock; jade pivot

Junction point
connecting front
and back meridians

Second lock; junction point
for macrocosmic orbit as it
enters from arms

Middle *dan tian*

Navel

Lower *dan tian*

Gate of life

First lock

Sea of qi point; junction point
for macrocosmic orbit as it
enters and returns from legs;
junction point for front and
back meridians

The microcosmic orbit

Living in silence, reading sacred books, exercising, having a regulated diet, taking herbs, and meditating gave Saihung a deep inner contentment. He never experienced claustrophobia. His all-consuming task and the strength of his inner vision opened up new vistas. His world had turned inward and, as he had seen with the Yin Immortal, the inner world could be infinite.

Completing the microcosmic orbit and continuing its practice did not make him superhuman. Rather, it was the cultivation of human potential. He felt extraordinarily vigorous. At this point, the manuals stated, he was on his way to developing the "golden body"—a healthy mind and body nearly impervious to illness and natural calamity.

On the afternoon of the forty-ninth day, he sat breathing the clear mountain air. He had completed his task. Although it had been a difficult one, he felt the rewards. He had changed, made his breakthrough. Saihung was elated.

Sunlight was streaming through the top half of the door when his master appeared. There was a smiling exchange of greetings as the Grand Master broke the seal and released him. Saihung spoke for the first time in weeks and recounted his experiences. The Grand Master nodded in approval.

The two of them left the meditation hut and hiked through the mountains. Huashan's natural beauty flooded Saihung's mind once again. Breathtaking vistas of rock, pine, and cloud, accented by falling water and pleasant breezes, combined to offer him joyful congratulations. He treasured his achievement, and it was his alone.

The master took his disciple through a gate on the East Peak and into the Two Immortals Cave. In its depths, Saihung would receive his vision.

The Two Immortals were two boys who had been playful acolytes on Huashan. As they romped along a path one morning, they had met a stout, muscular, white-haired man dressed in peasant clothing. Slung over his shoulder was a branch, with several enormous peaches.

He was Dong Fengshui, a disciple of the Northern Sea Immortal. Before he had become a disciple, he had been a thief. The impulses of his former profession had been difficult to suppress. Anxious to attain immortality, weary of austerities, and impatient with internal alchemy, he had gone to the garden of the Queen of the West and had stolen some peaches of immortality. He was just returning when he happened on the two boys.

He liked them immediately and spent the day playing with them. Intrigued by their wit and intelligence, he asked them complex riddles, and to his surprise the boys solved them with ease and flair.

"Little ones," Dong Fengshui addressed them as he stood to go. "I like you, but have nothing to give you in parting. How about taking one of these peaches? One bite and you shall live forty thousand years."

The boys clapped their hands delightedly and, after the man left, ate the entire peach. They instantly became immortal and their spirits ascended to heaven.

The Jade Emperor was surprised by their sudden appearance.

"How is it that two boys have acquired immortality?" asked the Emperor.

"A stranger gave us a magic peach," they answered.

"Ahhh, the stars must have been right for you to have such fortune," said the Jade Emperor. He ordered his ministers to investigate. They returned with a thorough account and confirmed that the Book of Life listed the two boys as predestined for immortality.

"I sanction your attainment," decreed the Jade Emperor. "Since you became immortal as children, you will remain children forever. And since you are such good friends, you shall be known as the Two Immortals." He touched their third eyes, opening them to perception, and bestowed divine wisdom on them. Then he gave them special scriptures and bade them return to earth to teach humanity.

The Two Immortals returned to Huashan and lived in the very cave Saihung now entered with his master. The Taoists believed that the psychic energy they left there, or perhaps their actual presence, would aid in other acolytes' quests.

Deep and wide, the cave was a tunnel filled with stalactites and stalagmites that had grown one by one over the centuries. Their eerie, grotesque shapes glowed with luminous minerals. It was a cave of eternal night lit only by iridescent pinnacles.

Saihung carried a torch, and its undulating flame cast jagged shadows. In spite of its light, Saihung could see no limits to the cave. But as they walked through the rock formations that dwarfed them, he saw a faint, skittering reflection. It was an underground river—an indigo mirror that doubled the stalactite ceiling—and so deep and mighty that it seldom rippled.

They went aboard a split bamboo raft that was in readiness at the bank. Saihung stuck his torch at the head of the raft and, taking up a long pole, pushed off.

Only the sound of his pole broke the silence. They went deep into the earth, where the rock smothered all sounds, where the river flowed on in complete quiet like a giant artery.

The river branched off into many different caves, but the Grand Master set an unerring course. The effect of the torch, shadows, reflections, and glowing rocks was mesmerizing and their frail craft was engulfed in a tunnel of whirling colors.

They disembarked at a grotto. Walking to its end, about fifty paces from the water's edge, they came to a large stone couch. The sides were carved with strange anthropomorphic figures and an indecipherable cursive script. The Grand Master gestured. Saihung put down animal skins and his prayer rug and lay down.

The Grand Master directed him into the proper position for dreaming. Saihung lay on his left side with his head resting on the crook of his left elbow with the hand cupping his ear. The right hand cupped his genitals. His left leg was straight, his right one bent with the ankle resting on his left knee. He would await his vision in this position.

The Grand Master left. He would return the next morning to bring Saihung back and interpret the vision. Until then Saihung was to sleep, and dream.

Everyone who had laid on that couch had had a vision; it was a certainty. The visions revealed different things. Some dreamers learned that they should go no further in ascetic training but should return to society. Others were shown a horrible future crisis they had to face. Some were given a special task. But no matter what came, both the acolyte and his master were bound to accept the omen. In most cases, the personal vision became the lodestone of the adept's life. It was a treasure, a jewel that shone only for him and guided him through the darkness of life.

Saihung lay still and quiet. His breathing became slow and regular. Mystery enveloped him and he fell swiftly asleep.

The next morning, his master appeared on the indigo waters, poling the frail raft alone. Saihung told him his vision. The Grand Master nodded.

"This is your vision, Saihung. It is the climax to years of effort. Tell no one of it. It is your secret source, the inspiration that will guide you in your future life of austerity and sustain you in times of adversity."

TWENTY-ONE

Learning Herbalism

SAIHUNG WENT to live in a compound with other adepts of his age and level of accomplishment. Although he still participated in the communal maintainence of the community, his only task was religious study. He read many sacred books and scriptures, continued to train his body, learned healing, and mastered more complex meditations.

The compound was a quadrangle of buildings, set on one side of a spacious mud-walled enclosure, within a large horseshoe-shaped meadow. This setting was itself within a granite basin. Old pines grew from crevices in the stone walls, and an abundant spring splashed down a gully of broken rock. Calligraphy was carved high on the cliff face. A number of meditation caves were visible on the high stone wall.

Several priests presided over the compound and supervised the students. They taught during the day and held discussions at night about scriptures, past Taoists, or the progress of the students.

Each adept had his own master and particular individual training. Their masters came periodically to instruct them. But the compound was to teach them certain basic subjects, giving them companionship and mutual support. A strong camaraderie existed among all the boys.

Medicine—one of the most important group subjects—was taught by Master Shifting Wind. He was a thin man with dark sunburned skin, silver hair, and large eyes black as onyx. He moved lightly and delicately and reminded Saihung of a deer more than anything else. Master Shifting Wind ate a diet of herbs and only a handful of rice. He approached his work reverently by worshipping Shen Nong daily before class at a shrine in his herb room. When he taught, he indicated that he possessed an amazing store of knowledge. He never used books—he had memorized them all. Medicine was based on the knowledge of organs, meridians, and body structures. It was the perfect complement to meditation. The meditations were concerned with points within the body, and medicine simultaneously improved visualization while teaching healing.

This was a fundamental hallmark of Chinese medicine: self-knowledge preceded giving knowledge to others. Just as the Emperor Shen Nong had experimented with herbs on his own body, so the aspiring adept also observed the effects of medicine on himself. Saihung's knowledge of massage, herbalism, and acupuncture was always based on experience with others and on his own experience as a patient.

Saihung's studies began with massage, since this skill was simply one body dealing with another. He learned that even with intermediate tools such as herbs and needles, direct healing was medicine in its most fundamental form. The most knowledgeable healers used only meditation, and thus beginners and sages were equal.

Massage familiarized Saihung with anatomy, pressure points, and meridians. He learned to project his *qi* into his fingers to strengthen his grip, and the ideal was to control his patient completely and relax him by the methodical grasping of the spots. If the patient was reluctant, tense, or apprehensive, Saihung used methods to open immediately the muscles and bones, making the body receptive to the kneading, slapping, or pressing treatments.

A wide range of illnesses could be healed with massage. He learned to treat dislocated and broken bones, bruises, some hemorrhages, muscle spasms, twisted veins, poisons in the bloodstream, clots, twisted nerves, neuralgia, and dislocated organs. He even saw his teachers cure a few mild cases of muscular dystrophy.

The second stage of massage required learning to project *qi* directly into a patient's body, and it was frustratingly difficult.

Projecting *qi* could bring deep poisons or clotted blood to the skin surface for dispersal or, as a life force transfusion, could save a life. Saihung experienced its feeling when the teacher demonstrated on him. An electrical field of prickly heat penetrated his skin. But when he tried this on a classmate, he could not make the energy rush forth. Master Shifting Wind instructed Saihung to leave his hands on his classmate, and then the Master put his own hands on Saihung's shoulderblades. Using Saihung's arms as conductors, he projected his *qi* through to the classmate. Saihung felt a surge of energy pass through his arms, and the master told him to try to reproduce the feeling to make his own *qi* come forth.

Diagnosis, an essential tool of medicine, was accomplished primarily through interpreting the pulse. This alone was a ten-year study. Diagnostic pulse reading was an outgrowth of the holistic view of the human body. Positing that the five organs and six viscera determined health, the physicians found that the organ's conditions could be read in the six different pulses at each wrist.

These pulses could be differentiated only by great sensitivity, subtle nuances of pressure, and by projecting *qi* through the healer's fingertips and into the bloodstream. His *qi* entered the body almost as a sonar, so that the echo of his own energy and the way it bounced back helped him reach his diagnosis. He used the "Eight Standards" in analyzing the state of each organ and viscera. By determining whether its condition was Yin or Yang, Hard or Soft, Inner or Outer, Hot or Cold, or a combination, he tried to ascertain the illness.

The teacher first took the pulse of the subject and then asked each student to diagnose. Master Shifting Wind, was strict. A system that demanded such a sensitive balance between subjectivity and objectivity inevitably led to many student mistakes. In his severity, Master Shifting Wind accused them repeatedly of lying or fantasizing. As he was a martial artist, his slaps were stinging. Saihung could not remember having heard himself called a turtle's egg or having been slapped so frequently even in his youth.

Saihung learned herbalism in an equally thorough way. Master Shifting Wind gave him picture books and a list and sent him out to pick them. On those trips, Saihung, dressed in a side-buttoning tunic, pants, and sandals, and wearing a rattan hat as broad as his shoulders, carried a hoe, sack, gourd, and knife. Although there were also overnight class field trips, Saihung and his classmates usually gathered herbs individually.

Once they returned, the herbs were cleaned, sorted, and prepared. Master Shifting Wind told each herb's history, what parts could be used, and how it was to be processed. Some were hung to dry and gave off a rich aromatic smell. Some were pulverized. Others were cooked, or ground into powders, and many roots were either crushed or sliced. Storage methods

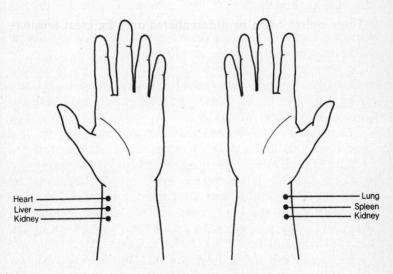

Heart
Liver
Kidney

Lung
Spleen
Kidney

The points for pulse diagnosis

were also precise and a variety of metal, porcelain, clay, or wood containers were used.

The herbs were used in combinations of ten to twelve different ingredients so that all parts of the body were treated. There was no such thing as treating just the ailing part because the Taoist physicians saw the body as a balanced, interrelated system. An herbal tea to cure a cold, for example, might have had one herb that entered the lung, another that stopped coughing, one that opened the lung meridian, another that cleared the head, one that the cleansed the bowels, and so on. By the careful mixture of ingredients from any one of 8,000 documented herbs, the Chinese physician was able to deal with the most subtle peculiarities of an illness.

The Taoists did not like to treat illness; they preferred to prevent it with tonic herbs. Medical classics stated that treating an illness after it had begun was like "waiting until one is thirsty to dig a well" or "suppressing a revolution after it has begun." Saihung was familiar with preventive medicine all through his apprenticeship. But in serious cases, the doctors could choose acupuncture, surgery, healing with talismans, and (the highest and most dramatic type of healing Saihung witnessed) healing with the mind.

One day, a portly man was admitted to Huashan. He was dying. He had a bluish pallor, and a tongue so swollen that it threatened to choke him.

The man was an extraordinarily rich aristocrat and yet had been unable to find a doctor to save him. In desperation, he ordered himself carried to Huashan and begged for help.

Master Shifting Wind went to see him. He diagnosed the symptoms as poisoning and after questioning the man, surmised that a rival must have done it. "You will either choke to death, or, if the poison reaches your heart, die of a heart attack," he concluded.

The Taoists decided to heal him. Master Shifting Wind sat behind the aristocrat, laying his hands on the man's back. He was in constant concentration for two hours until he suddenly fell over. His face was pale, he could not move, and his palms were black.

Two other doctors dragged him to a stone. Master Shifting Wind drew himself up and placed his hands on the rock to expel the poison. Two black handprints were left there when he was done. The stone was buried.

He was exhausted and was sealed in a shrine for three months of meditation in order to regenerate his life force. The patient survived, and both he and the master recovered with normal herb therapy.

Saihung deeply admired the master's sacrifice. It was an inspiration and high standard. He still thought often of the physician's simple dedication and tried to apply it to his own life. After he entered into another regimen of meditation and gained greater skill, he was constantly reminded of his teacher's selflessness.

TWENTY-TWO

Awakening the Body Centers

ONE OF THE HIGHEST meditations that Saihung learned, the *ling qiu* meditation, opened the psychic centers. The body centers, situated in a straight line from the base of the body to the top of the head, had specific healing and spiritual powers. Meditation aimed at bringing the life force straight up through each of the centers to the crown. Paralleling the Indian Kundalini meditation, the Taoists opened each of the centers until, at the very top, they reached what the Hindus called Samadhi, the Buddhists called Nirvana, and the Taoists called Stillness. Saihung began to practice the attainment of that Immortal Spirit.

Each center, according to its anatomical placement, controlled and healed the adjacent body structures and organs and yielded particular psychic powers. The Grand Master continually warned Saihung that the abilities that would come to him would be gifts from the gods and were not to be abused. Many ascetics, having come this far, had fallen because they had grown obsessed with the importance of their centers. Instead of reaching the spiritual, they remained fascinated with the use of their lower centers and became trapped in the abuse of their powers.

Before he meditated to awaken each center, Saihung studied that center's colors and response to invocation, and looked at a diagram of its shape. Each center was imagined as a lotus bud that could be opened by the specific sound of the invocation. Within the flower was a certain pattern of colors. While he concentrated on that pattern in meditation, Saihung produced the invocation. The blooming center lit up and its powers began to emanate. Saihung felt whirling sensations and heat whenever the center was activated. When the meditation was complete, the center closed and became dormant again.

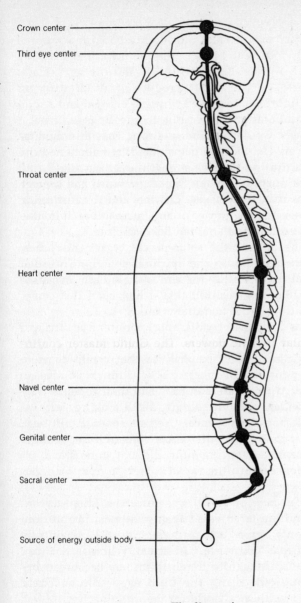

Crown center

Third eye center

Throat center

Heart center

Navel center

Genital center

Sacral center

Source of energy outside body

The ling qui

The first center was actually outside the body and was the source of energy. Saihung brought the life force into his body at the base of his spine. Both this center and the next one at the navel controlled life and reproduction. Meditating on them brought lightness, increased physical energy, and sexual desire. The Grand Master warned him that feelings of physical and sexual power would become so strong that he might be reluctant to go on. He said that many adepts remained at those two centers, cultivating massive strength and sexuality for all sorts of deviant purposes. When Saihung opened the centers, he found it was true. Deep sexual cravings and the realization that he could develop the power of an almost unbeatable martial artist tempted him and strained his discipline.

As soon as he opened the solar plexus center, his ordeal ceased. He had passed into the spiritual centers. The solar plexus was a source of vitality for him and gave him increased power to heal. Saihung realized that it had been this center that Master Shifting Wind had drawn on.

The heart was compassion, skill, appreciation of beauty, and artistry. Opening it developed artistic ability and supported the arts. The Grand Master emphasized that creativity arose from this center and that people like Mist Through a Grove, an unusually talented musician, naturally had theirs open.

The throat center, not surprisingly, aided singing, but was also responsible for clairvoyance. Used in combination with the third eye, it interpreted the perceptions of other realities seen by that center. Often Saihung did not understand his spiritual experiences until the throat center poured forth verbal understanding.

The upper *dan tian*, or third eye, perceived other dimensions. The Grand Master stressed again that most people, and Saihung, had only agreed to see the world in a certain way and had called that "existence." In actuality, it was not real. Reality was the shifting of different illusions, because many dimensions coexisted. Using the third eye, Saihung could pierce through the illusory world for the meaning behind it.

Ascending the body centers symbolized the whole of Sai-hung's training. He had developed his body powers; learned martial arts; secured his health, longevity, and vitality; become versed in art, literature, science, and divination; and had perceived extrasensory realities and spiritual wisdom.

Now he entered his final center. He was on the threshold of a level that was at once a culmination of many arduous years and the foundation for higher states: the crown center. The thousand-petal lotus bloomed. His senses dropped away. There was no external reality, no internal reality. He felt nothing, thought nothing. He merged completely with voidness.

TWENTY-THREE

A Chance at Immortality

AT DAWN a fine mist floated over the meadow, settling into silvery beads on the tile roofs of the compound. The birds usually sang high-pitched warbles even before light, but today the air was still, almost deathly in its silence.

Saihung and his classmates were drawing water from the spring. The heavy, opaque air made it impossible even to see the gate, and they simply bent wordlessly to the task. The water splashed him. It was clear, but so cold that it stung.

Saihung felt a tap on his shoulder. A classmate gestured. He looked. A tall figure walked slowly across the yard.

The man was a Taoist, dressed traditionally. Even more than others, though, he was wrapped completely in an air of total aloofness. His feet may have been in this world, but his spirit seemed already to be floating in the other. His gait was so light that he seemed not to touch the ground. Saihung strained to see through the diaphanous air, and he saw the lump on the man's forehead. It was Master Sun the Immortal, whom he had glimpsed only once from a distance seven years before.

They hurried inside, where Master Sun stood speaking with the priests. The students assembled and bowed, and Master Sun walked among them, examining each one.

In the dawn light, Saihung saw Master Sun closely for the first time. The strands of his white hair were coarse, almost wiry. The hair was coiled neatly, the beard hung like a veil. His skin was slightly wrinkled, his nose aquiline, his lips thin and sharply sculpted. The lump on his forehead was grotesquely tumorous.

There was no sound when he walked. His robes were so

heavy and bulky that Saihung thought he might not have feet at all. Master Sun stopped before him, pointed, and then continued.

In all, he picked three acolytes. While Master Sun stood at the door, the priests explained.

"Master Sun the Immortal has truly attained immortality," said the head priest, "and he seldom comes to the temples. This is one rare time. You three have been selected from all of Huashan as eligible to become his disciples. But if you go, you will be true renunciates. You will never see the human world again."

Saihung thought hard. He had a chance to be immortal! But actually to live forever was a sobering thought. Did he really want to? First, he felt no affinity for Master Sun, whereas he loved his own master. Second was Master Sun's appearance. He was one of the few Taoists who permitted no loss of sperm, not even in his urine, and it had to go somewhere. The lump was formed from the accumulation of *jing*, and Master Sun undoubtedly had many other lumps on his body.

"If you are ready, step forward and leave the world," said the priest.

"No," thought Saihung. "I'm not ready yet. And the gods know I'm ugly enough already. Who wants to live forever ugly with lumps all over? It would be better just to learn spirituality."

Saihung did not step forward, but the other two did. He watched them disappear with Master Sun as they walked into the thick mist. They never looked back, and Saihung never saw them again.

TWENTY-FOUR

War

NEWS OF THE Sino-Japanese War in 1937 came to Huashan with the monthly supplies. The students who had gone down for provisions had rushed back up the mountain with the report that Japan had swept across the Marco Polo Bridge outside of Beijing, overrun the iron- and coal-rich northern mountains of Shaanxi Province, and had begun a second drive from Tianjin toward Nanjing. Attacking at their own pace, the Japanese had advanced steadily into the Chinese countryside, meeting emotional but badly organized and poorly supplied resistance. The disunited warlord armies and the civilian population of the northern provinces had been crushed by superbly trained, tank-led, air-supported columns.

The exceptionally gruesome stories of the fighting and atrocities shocked everyone, including Saihung. Resentment and hatred fueled nationalism, and controversy spread to all the temples of Huashan. Every priest, acolyte, and student had a different opinion. Some were excited and emotional, others calm and aloof, but all condemned the war. Daily routines were disturbed, and soon the Taoists of Huashan did not need to read of the war but instead saw it in the distance: they heard the bombing, watched fighter planes overhead, and saw dull red flashes give rise to fattening columns of black smoke as the Japanese attacked Xian sixty miles away.

A large number of Taoists advocated noninvolvement in the war. They insisted that they as ascetics, "people-who-had-left-their-families," should not return to worldly affairs and break the purity they had so long cultivated. The world was a place of war, deceit, dishonesty, money, killing, politics, and danger. They did not want to break their ascetic commitment.

Patriotic Taoists disagreed, saying that if China was overrun or destroyed, ascetics would have no place to practice their arts. Moved by indignation and righteousness, these people urged some involvement. Renunciates or not, they were needed by their country and people.

Controversy split the community until the Grand Master called a public assembly. All the priests and students from Huashan's five peaks came in steady streams. Many engaged in heated discussions as they crowded anxiously into the courtyards of the South Peak Temple to await the Grand Master's instruction.

He walked out to the portico of the main hall, his tall figure standing out against the ancient wooden temple. Lifting an old, battered megaphone to his lips, the Grand Master addressed them in a high pitched, authoritative voice.

"We are Taoist renunciates. We have all left the world and should remain unconcerned with the insignificant and petty squabbles of small-minded men. Entering the world again is to forsake the purity we have cultivated on this holy mountain: it is impossible to be in the world and remain untainted.

"Yet we are also Chinese. A foreign power is invading our country and every person must do his part in defending it. There is more to life than spirituality.

"Aiding the war effort need not mean fighting. Each man must contribute in his own way; each man must ask himself how he can best help China. Some may go down and feed the people, some should give medical aid, and some should properly preserve the ancient traditions for the future. Even if you will not kill, you can still contribute.

"For those of you trained in the martial traditions, you must defend in that way. You are warriors, and the business of a warrior is war. . . . "

The Grand Master continued his speech, but Saihung's mind was already racing. He was young and outraged. He wanted to defend his people and homeland. He wanted to seek revenge for the atrocities committed against helpless people. He wanted to fight.

That evening he and the two acolytes discussed the future.

"We have been trained thoroughly. Our martial skills are unusual," said Saihung passionately. "We must offer our skills to our country."

His two former guardians listened seriously. Mist Through a Grove rarely expressed his inner feelings and Sound of Clear Water, though outspoken, was equally taciturn about his personal decisions. There was a long period of silence after Saihung had stopped talking. Sound of Clear Water simply announced that he was leaving the mountain.

"We are martial artists. We fight," said Sound of Clear Water. "When I think of the inhuman acts forced upon women, children, and the elderly, I cannot contain myself. I cannot stand by. I shall kill."

"And I, too," said Saihung.

They turned to Mist Through a Grove. He said nothing, but returned their look steadily. He had not argued. They knew he would go.

"It is impossible to fight and be in the sect," continued Saihung. "It will be impossible to keep the precepts on the battlefield. I shall be entangled in the world. I am leaving the sect."

"Saihung," said Mist Through a Grove. "You musn't abandon your path."

"I'll become a wandering Taoist unaffiliated with a temple. Look, sometimes I can't stand it up here. I never have enough to eat, and training seven days a week can be depressing. Every day, it's wake up and recite sutras; eat breakfast, recite sutras; eat lunch, recite sutras; eat dinner, recite sutras; go to sleep, recite sutras. I tell you, I'd rather be a lone ascetic."

"You took your vows," Sound of Clear Water reminded him.

"I know. I remain a Taoist. But even if I could recite sutras on the battleground, it would be hypocritical. I'll be scheming, fighting for my life, eating meat, thinking evil, killing. How can I honor the precepts? I need all my energy and strength to concentrate on fighting."

The two acolytes glanced at each other.

"Do as you like, Saihung," said Mist Through a Grove. "But I shall try to keep the precepts."

"I shall, as well," said Sound of Clear Water.

"How can you?" asked Saihung hotly. "You'll be killing. Don't the priests say that those who kill shall be punished in hell?"

"They say," stressed the Sound of Clear Water, "that to kill another human being is a sin. Would human beings commit those atrocities?"

"Besides, Saihung," added Mist Through a Grove, "we must fight evil and defend ourselves. We do not kill for pleasure, but we've all fought bandits and animals who have attacked us on the mountain. Even holy men must defend themselves. We have been attacked without provocation. It is our right to defend ourselves."

The next day, Saihung went to see his master. He was dressed not in his robes but in black martial artist's clothing bound at the wrists and ankles. He bowed and requested permission to enter. The Grand Master nodded a silent acknowledgment.

"I'm leaving the mountain," said Saihung.

The Grand Master's eyes narrowed. Before he could reply, Saihung swiftly added, "and I'm leaving the sect."

The Grand Master slammed his palm loudly to the desk. He glared angrily at him. It was the first time Saihung had seen his master angry, and he was surprised.

"You and your saucy mouth! Think! Don't speak carelessly with me!" shouted the Grand Master.

"I cannot keep the precepts on the battlefield."

"Who says you're going? You cannot just do as you please! Where did you get such impudent ideas? You are not to run around following your ridiculous whims; you are supposed to follow your training."

"But I must fight. If I fight, I must eat."

"The precepts must be observed!"

"You say the body is the temple of the gods," said Saihung

defiantly. "Am I to fight without nourishment? What will happen to the 'temple' then? The body must be nourished. The gods won't remain in an ill-repaired temple."

"You are filled with unwholesome ideas. You're too presumptuous!"

"If the mind is not allowed to be independent, we're no better than vegetables."

The Grand Master stood up and fixed Saihung with a stern look. "Youngster! You're young and know no better. A little learning and you are ready to tell the world what to do. Think carefully before you take this irresponsible plunge."

"I am becoming a wandering Taoist," replied Saihung steadily. "I am going and won't be tied to a temple."

"If you leave," said his master sharply, "don't come back!"

Saihung was stunned. But there was nothing more to be said. "*Da Shi*, I am leaving."

The Grand Master sat down and simply waved him away in dismissal.

The adepts of Huashan were famous for their martial abilities and were eagerly accepted into the warlord armies. Saihung and the two acolytes separated, and each entered guerrilla units that had no restrictions on movement. The conventional armies were limited by the rules of war, but Saihung's units under Cai Tingjie and Bai Songqi fought in any way they pleased. Often they roamed behind enemy lines or acted as advance scouts, harassing, sabotaging, and gathering intelligence information against the enemy. Skilled and capable, Saihung and his expert unit preferred traditional weapons and carried guns only when they joined an army for conventional warfare.

Saihung's primary weapons were a single-edged saber and a spear. He dressed completely in black cotton clothes tied at the wrists and ankles, walked on straw sandals, and coiled his braided hair beneath a black cloth wrapping. He was a fiery and idealistic soldier, as energetic but as temperamental as a stallion. He specialized in isolated attacks, picking off men one by one. Attacking at dawn, twilight, or even in broad daylight, Saihung hid in tall grass and became expert at killing passing soldiers. He pierced throats with his spear so that his victims died soundlessly.

In close-range fighting, he favored the saber. Saihung lured enemy soldiers close to himself so that they were forced to depend on bayonets and knives rather than on bullets. In that situation, Saihung's eight-pound saber, honed by blades in the scabbard each time it was drawn, was a superior weapon. With whirling motions and mighty leaps, Saihung parried with ease, using the momentum to sever limbs in single swings. He remembered the philosophy of his saber instructors about piercing, slashing, parrying, and hacking: a shallow cut is used to torture a victim, decapitation is merciful.

Saihung released all the power of his youth and training in hand combat. His palms were devastating, his kicks had an iron hardness. His meridians were opened, his internal energy was conserved by celibacy, and his techniques were forged by his spartan training. He was a wild fighter. It became easy for him to dispatch a man with a single strike or break a neck with a simple twist.

His idealism slowly wore away in the climate of warfare, and Saihung found himself motivated by something new: hatred. The intellect grew dumb on the battlefield, and compassion was lost in the stark contrasts of wartime realities. He had learned many things on Huashan but it was not until he saw enemy atrocities with his own eyes that he learned to hate men. Whenever he entered villages abandoned by the enemy, he saw bloody testimonials to human depravity. Torn bodies left mute histories of raped women, whipped flesh, bayonetted babies, mutilated boys, staked and burned genitals. The horror became so redundant that his eyes grew weary. But for his heart and will the repetition was constant refueling of a fire that forged hatred in him and sharpened it to a razor's edge. The war atrocities seared his companions' souls of all sensitivity; they fought firmly and stoically. Not so with Saihung. He lived from day to day, powered by a flickering alternation between commitment to his cause and pure madness.

Battle after battle shook his psyche. He was wounded and scarred in body and mind by sounds that always seemed like questions. They haunted him. The ominous thuds of exploding bombs, the mad percussion of machine-gun fire, even the whisper of flesh parted from flesh as his blade made its absolute division were familiar though still chilling. But it was when human sounds reached him—the anonymous whimper of a frightened child, the scream of a dying comrade, the last moan of his enemy—that he felt the sound addressed his soul directly. He yearned for those rare moments when the battlefield was quiet. In those fleeting moments, the sounds of warfare that all asked the question "Why?" faded. But he then took up the refrain within himself. During lulls in the cacophony of destruction, he tried to sort out his own thoughts and resolve the apparently monstrous dichotomy between Taoism and the war.

The purity of Huashan was undeniable, its focus on asceticism strict and absolute. There was no temptation, if only because little opportunity existed on the peaks to practice sin. It was a community of dedicated individuals, and, whether saint or beginning acolyte, all were completely given over to spirituality. The most there was to hate was the dull regularity of monastic life.

Huashan seemed like heaven compared to the filth and degradation of the battlefield, where both the mountain and heaven seemed distant and inaccessible. Now he lived a wretched life of anger, killing, and intrigue. He had to steal his food, eating whatever he could scrounge, and poured his intelligence into setting traps. He had to put his spirituality completely aside in order to throw the totality of his being into slaughtering other men. The old Taoists were right. It was impossible to live in the world without being entangled.

But for the time being he *was* fully entangled. Each time he saw the mounds of rotten flesh that were feasts for the dogs and crows, his passion welled up for revenge. Battle cries drowned out the whispers of scriptures. Fury pushed aside morality. He had to fight to save his people. Since childhood he had been told that to kill was to incur eternal damnation. He accepted it. He would go to hell with no regrets.

At times, his thoughts of Huashan became bitter and cynical. If the Taoists were so great, why didn't they stop the war? But each time he could also answer himself in the words he had so often heard: The Taoists were renunciates. The world was not real; the world did not matter.

But weren't they men? Weren't they Chinese? Couldn't they stop the senseless assaults with their extraordinary powers? He realized soberly that even if they could, they wouldn't. Every person had his destiny, everyone had to choose between good and evil, and humanity had to find its own way from savagery to divinity. War was destiny, and destiny was inescapable even for the gods. Spirituality offered no obvious way out. The renunciates remained on the mountain, others struggled on the plains. But spirituality was only human aspiration crystalized. It could not work miracles. The Taoists, Saihung realized sadly, were only men after all.

Ordinary human beings. It was true that they had turned their backs on the self-destructive and self-indulgent tragedies most people called their lives. A person on the Taoist path sought his own liberation, secured it, and tried to help others all he could to gain their liberation too. But humanity was composed of individuals, each one born with the same free will and opportunity of choice between sacrificing for higher consciousness or plunging toward degradation. That was the human task. That was human meaning, individualized. If there were no evil, there would be no consequence and thus no choice. Humanity always had a choice, and ultimately one's freedom could be attained only by one's persistent conscious effort. The Taoists could not rescue all of a nation nor the whole planet. That would have been an act of grace. Divine intervention of that sort was beyond the power of even the Jade Emperor himself.

Saihung's contemplations gave him perspective. He thought of reincarnation. Human life was the halfway point between upper and lower states of consciousness: humanity had not yet resolved this dilemma in its evolutionary progression. The war, as activity during a moment of this evolution, suddenly seemed petty and insignificant.

But these philosophical flights were taking place on a battlefield. He was here. Death surrounded him, the dichotomy and the dilemma could not be resolved. He had to go on now. He didn't want to die; he didn't want to be killed. Despite his introspection into moral considerations, he formulated a simple conclusion. He would kill anyone who tried to kill him. Only then could he succeed in his present task.

TWENTY-FIVE

Homecoming

L IVING AS A WARRIOR was not complete horror. Saihung traveled through all of China, from Beijing to Guangdong, from Henan to Sichuan. Even warfare could not obscure the enduring beauty and tremendous variations in the Chinese landscape. Whenever armies passed or joined together he looked for his friends, periodically enjoying reunions with the two acolytes. Sometimes the surprise of good fortune relieved terrible burdens by gifting him with a peaceful moment or the rare appearance of a chicken. Then Saihung and his comrades laughed happily as they roasted the bird in local clay to make "Beggar's Chicken." Meals like that were like snatchings from a heavenly banquet, and spring water became as sweet as thousand-year-old wine.

Missions were not always against the Japanese either. Saihung and his men, in one assignment, cheerfully attacked Chiang Kaishek himself.

The nationalist Generalissimo was fond of taking hostages to ensure his own generals' loyalty or to punish them. In the Xian incident, he had taken the teenage son of one of the generals leading the northern armies.

Saihung's commander, the general Cai Tingjie, resented this and saw in the imprisonment certain death for the teenager. Civil war would begin again, and the northern armies were sure to split off from the Nationalists. Cai Tingjie instructed Saihung's unit to go to Nanjing and free the hostage. Even though the plan represented insubordination and treason, the general sent them off quietly with the words, "Do it, just on the side."

Once in Nanjing, the group consulted underworld spies and informers, easily obtaining a general layout of Chiang's residence. Chiang Kaishek was a careful man. His palatial residence was surrounded by high walls, numerous troops, and personal body guards. The spies doubted whether anyone could penetrate the Generalissimo's defenses.

It was a challenge, and Saihung loved to respond to challenges. He and his men formulated a plan to be put into effect a few days later, when the moon would be new.

When that dark night came, Saihung and a partner hid in shrubbery outside the gardens where the young prisoner was kept. At the prearranged moment, the other men, pretending to be drunk, began a brawl with the guards on the other side of the estate. Saihung and his friend quickly scaled the walls, dropped silently into the garden and reached the bordering walkway. They could see lights go on and heard much shouting as men rushed toward the fight.

Two men remained posted at the entrance to the targeted building. Saihung stole up and, using the Snake style, struck their pressure points. The guards pitched forward. Saihung unlocked the doors and entered the long hallway.

There was no way of knowing how many guards were inside the building or behind which doors they might be. It was a tense moment when they stepped gingerly onto the carpeted floor. Stalking the length of the hallway, they inched forward within the darkened house.

A faint flickering light signaled the presence of two more guards. This time there was no surprise attack, but a desperate scuffle. Saihung struggled frantically with them until he dispatched them. His companion broke the locked door, and they found the boy.

Returning to Xian, Saihung and his group returned the son to his father. The northern armies were relieved. Chiang Kaishek had no means of extortion now, and they were assured that Chiang would keep his promise to stop civil war and enter fully into the war against Japan. He must have been furious at the loss of his hostage, but he was much too shrewd to let it show. Yet everyone in the northern armies, including the

general and his son, enjoyed much laughter at the Generalissimo's expense.

Two years of war life, whether horror or adventure, began
to wear on Saihung. His training and a certain acquired ruth-
lessness had preserved him thus far. But as the war reached a
frustrating stalemate, he began assessing the situation and
thinking of his future.

By 1939, military conflict had reached a standoff when the
Chinese, driven into the heartland by the advancing Japanese,
had entrenched themselves in tenuous lines along the foothills and valley rims. Supporting industry had been reestab-
lished behind these lines. The Japanese attacked the perimeter
of these lines in small battles designed to train their own
troops, terrorize the countryside, and keep the Chinese disor-
ganized. They struck deep into the fronts, marauding and
plundering before turning back. The Chinese responded by retreating, then attempting to pinch off the withdrawing Japanese units. But they could never destroy the superbly fortified
Japanese garrisons, and a wide zone of desolation developed
between the two forces. The Japanese returned again and
again. Town after town was razed, peasants died by the thousands, and the dry soil was soaked with blood.

Saihung grew tired. Men were entrenched in foxholes
dumbly awaiting the next attack, nursing infected sores, and
expiring from fever. The war grew meaningless. He realized
that there was still a world beyond the war, and that he had
much to learn about that world. In Shandong Province, where
the Yellow River finally ends its journey to the sea, he decided
to disband his guerilla unit and strike back to Huashan, west-
ward in China's interior.

In the back of his mind, however, he was uncertain that he
would be welcomed on the mountain. When he had broken
away, his master had forbidden him to return. Saihung wondered whether he would be permitted reentry.

During that long trek to Huashan, he detoured toward the

Guan family mansion. He knew that his grandparents had first taken refuge on Huashan but that both his grandmother and his grandfather now lay ill in a woodcutter's hut. His father was fighting, the rest of his family had fled to the interior, and the Guan clan had scattered. He knew that the mansion had had to be abandoned, but he wanted to see it again. There was no one to greet him. He arrived at his ancestral home alone.

A seasoned veteran, he nevertheless felt a deep sorrow when he came to the ruins of his family structures. The dragon estate, the gardens and pavilions that had been the culmination of four generations of the Guan clan, lay shattered in the scorched fields.

It was evident that Japanese troops had occupied the mansion before either leaving or having been driven out. Bullet holes were scattered like black scars on lavender walls. Cannon fire had torn gaping holes in the sides of buildings. Violent blows had splintered fragile lattices. Fire had consumed pavilions and ancient trees. Poison had polluted the streams and wells. Horses had been stabled in the family chapel. All art objects had either been plundered or smashed.

A wan and pale light sifted through the wreckage, lighting up dozens of bodies. Some were of Japanese and Chinese soldiers, but most were of servants caught in the attack. The remains of people, some of whom Saihung had known since birth as vital personalities, now lay twisted and still. He saw the body of a raped boy, blood still encrusted on his loins. In the shadow was a young girl, hair tangled, teeth broken, legs bare. An old stableman still hung from the rafters, his flesh sliced from his body in dangling strips. On each and every corpse, the faces were frozen in the terror of their violent deaths, their eyes still uncomprehending of their last moments.

Saihung walked stoically through the courtyards and hallways, trying to replace the present with the past. It was useless. Putrid flesh overcame scents of incense and jasmine in places where families had strolled. The charred ruins that represented former slender polychromed columns were characteristic of the shell that had once protected the glory and vigor of a clan. Life would never rise again here. No future could breathe that would not be tainted by the smell of men and women who had been destroyed, unaided and unpitied.

He stood in the garden where Guan Jiuyin had played his flute. Now the fish lay belly up on the surface of the stagnant pond. His family home was no more. Saihung turned his back on it and left. It was useless to weep. It had been the will of heaven.

Saihung climbed up Huashan's steep trail. The air was still and cool, the light direct and clear. What a different place Huashan was! It was sacred. He felt acutely aware of the contrast between its austere serenity and the filth of the battlefield. Saihung stopped twice to wash himself in the mountain streams, but the bitterness and grime were hard to cleanse. He felt as if he were defiling the holy.

In humility he continued the climb toward his master. Perhaps he had never really appreciated Huashan. The first time he had been carried up and tricked. In subsequent times he had looked at it as a tedious boarding school. Even when he had returned for his initiation, his faith had been incomplete and his heart filled with doubt. Now, he had chosen to return, ready to commit himself to austerity and knowledge. Stained with blood, wracked with injury, he sought his solace, and the mountain seemed to accept him.

A group of monks saw him and came out to greet him. They happily exchanged their experiences. Some, due to their vows had not gone down. The rest had gone either to heal or to fight. Saihung inquired about his master. He suspected that the Grand Master's anger had been merely a formality but he mentioned it anyway.

The old temple cook burst out laughing.

"*Da Shi* disappears all the time," he said. "He doesn't say where he's going. He only says, 'I have business,' and is absent for months. We know that sometimes he went out and fought."

"How do you know?" asked Saihung.

"The newspaper clippings with the monthly supplies periodically mentioned an old Taoist with a cane. Only *Da Shi* carries that cane. We asked him about the news. Of course, he denied everything."

"What did the clippings say?"

"We know *Da Shi* went to Shanghai and Beijing to accept challenges from Japanese martial artists. The last time was in 1936."

"I was still here! Why didn't he take me?"

"Probably because your bad temper would have led you to jump in the ring yourself and get you killed."

"Oh."

"The Japanese called us 'Sick Men of the Orient,' and *Da Shi* went to accept their challenges. He defeated a sumo wrestler in Shanghai with two fingers to the throat. He used just his sleeves and palms in a Beijing match where two karate, an akido, and judo masters attacked him simultaneously."

"So *Da Shi* isn't above getting involved himself!" cried Saihung.

"Apparently not," returned the priest. "Then there was another time that this same Taoist appeared in Sichuan."

"Sichuan!" exclaimed Saihung. "What was he doing there?"

"Just so," said the priest dryly. "How do we know why *Da Shi* was there? There was a teahouse there occupied by Japanese troops. Their commander was reputedly fourth dan black belt in karate. Well, the old Taoist walked right in and nonchalantly sat down for tea. The frightened waiters didn't know what to do but serve him. The commander boasted of his skills and the inferiority of Chinese warriors, until the old Taoist put his teacup down and laughed mockingly. The commander attacked, but the old Taoist threw him with one hand. A big fight erupted, and only the Taoist walked out of the teahouse."

"That old windbag!" cursed Saihung. "Giving me that sham rebuke! I'm going to get even!"

"Better not, Saihung," chuckled the priest. "*Da Shi* always has the last laugh."

"That's true," admitted Saihung with an embarrassed smile. "He certainly did this time."

They came to the entrance of the South Peak Temple, and the monks all urged him in. Saihung sought his master and found him in the study. Saihung knelt down.

The Grand Master looked down at him noncommittally. Saihung saw that his master had not changed. The quiet observant eyes that could gaze unblinkingly, the snowy hair and beard, the upright posture were so familiar. Saihung waited for his master to speak.

"So you made it back?" inquired the Grand Master softly.

"Yes, *Da Shi*."

"Since you're here, you should begin the next stage of training."

That was all. The Grand Master accepted and dismissed him with a gentle wave.

PART FIVE

DISCOVERING
THE TRUE SELF

TWENTY-SIX

The Labyrinth

Aweek after his return, Saihung vowed before the gods to remain sealed in a cave practicing austerities until he made a breakthrough. The Grand Master selected an auspicious day and walked with him to the West Peak. They paused at the stone slab at the opening to the cave. His master turned to him and said, "This is the place where you will discover your true self."

They descended along a tunnel that was the entryway to a labyrinth of passages and chambers. Saihung would live in a cluster of five chambers deep in the mountain, where countless corridors and holes remained to be explored. They wound their way into the mazelike hollows. The air was immediately chilly; the only sounds were of their footsteps. At times, the passage narrowed so much that they had to inch through sideways. Some parts of the cave were smothered in darkness, others glowed with luminous minerals. There were stalactites, drooping as if the stone itself were fluid, descending to meet stalagmites that rose in piercing peaks. A wide stream flowed by them and led the way to the five chambers lit by torches and oil lamps.

Several of these chambers had natural holes in their ceilings, and these were not only vents for the coal-burning cast-iron warmer, but also admitted some sunlight. By the skylights and the torches, Saihung saw his few possessions: a stone bed, incense stand, oil lamp, books, water gourd, hourglass, musical instruments, writing utensils, diary, and another robe.

There was a separate chamber devoted solely to meditation. The stream ran into it, pooling deeply in its center before flowing on. A heavy wooden meditation platform standing on feet modeled as dragon claws and carved with ancient ciphers was flanked by two iron incense burners shaped like cranes. A perfect circle incised into the sand-covered stone floor consecrated the whole platform.

Saihung laid a grass mat, leopard skin, and prayer rug on the platform. The Grand Master gave him a *Ba Gua* mirror, tied a talisman around his neck, and gave him last-minute instructions.

"Many Taoists have gained their realization on this very spot," said his master as he turned to leave. "All your elders have preceded you here. Study and persevere, Saihung, and you too shall succeed."

Saihung watched the Grand Master flicker into the shadows. He was alone.

Each day was based on four practices: morning meditation, astral travel, sutra recitation, and evening meditation. Around that framework was time for three hot meals brought in by classmates, practice of martial arts, reading of scriptures, playing music, writing, painting, and exploring the cave.

Rising in the morning, Saihung ate his breakfast, bathed, and did body-cleansing and strengthening exercises before going to the meditation chamber. Sitting within the sacred circle, he drew a special diagram in the sand. The complex pattern of circles, squares, lines, and angles invoked all forces on heaven and earth, called forth the ten directions, and conjured the five elements. Every stroke was drawn with an invocation and each one represented a god. The laborious ritual put him into a state of contemplation and created a diagram that protected and supported him. Saihung stepped into its center and sat down.

Both the pattern and his talisman would guard his body against possession once his spirit left his body. Lacking this protection, Saihung's physical shell was vulnerable to the many evil spirits and demons who readily sought an available shell. They could enter any one of the nine apertures of the body and prevent the return of Saihung's spirit.

Now in a quiet state, Saihung performed a series of twenty-four prayer gestures—complex hand positions that isolated thought, deepened concentration, and prepared his spirit to leave his body. The gestures represented the whole course of evolution: Saihung's meditation was the imagined culmination of the creation of the very universe.

He felt wholly otherworldly. He quietly read the sutra laid on a stand before him. The words had power. They induced his journey.

He invoked the gods with the sutra. Saihung called out their names and visualized them before him until he had reconstructed the entire Taoist pantheon. All of heaven, headed by the Three Pure Ones, was before him.

His spirit left his body, mounted on a dragon, and ascended to heaven. Once there, he prostrated himself before the gods and sat in meditation awaiting instruction. On occasions when the gods did not speak, Saihung asked his own questions of the gods.

After two hours he repeated another part of the sutra and returned to consciousness. He ended by performing dispersing exercises, and erased the diagram stroke by stroke, each time reciting sutras to release the god called by the diagram.

Sutra reading could also be an act by itself. Before his noon meal each day, Saihung recited a sutra that appealed to the gods to purge the consequences of his past lives. The entire pantheon was invoked twice each day. The yang gods were called at noon, the yin gods in the evening.

At midday Saihung meditated again before free time in the afternoon when he explored the mysteries of the caverns.

The cave was a complex and irregular network that twisted around on many levels. Some parts were reached only by crawling through narrow tubes in the rock, swimming underwater, or walking across naturally formed stone bridges. Previous hermits sequestered in the caves had explored and noted many parts, but many sections were unknown and even considered dangerous. Some of the tunnels had stone plaques set above them warning against entering. Other passages were favorite places for Saihung, but when he ventured into the unfamiliar he frequently met with mysterious and sometimes frightening experiences.

Early in his stay he crawled down a rock vent and found a long corridor. Venturing several yards into it, he came on the opening of a shaft that plunged straight downward below the cave floor. Peering into the shaft, Saihung saw that ancient steps had been cut, and an iron chain pegged to the walls. Grasping his torch, Saihung began the descent.

He counted the steps as he made his way down. The light from the cave above quickly dwindled into a pale dot before disappearing entirely. His torch was his only light source. He went on counting.

The rhythm of his steps became hypnotic. The darkness was disorienting. Only the shaft, with its remarkably straight progression, presented any solid context. He counted past five hundred.

He paused at a thousand steps. He thought he heard a faint sound. One thousand two hundred. Was that a voice? One thousand three hundred. Definite voices. Strange muffled shrieks and cries. He looked upward. The darkness was absolute. His courage began to falter even as he crept down to step one thousand five hundred. He heard voices speaking in an unknown tongue. As he looked down, the steps and chain disappeared from sight. The voices approached him. Now thoroughly frightened, he climbed quickly back up. He did not stop until he reached the surface, panting.

He never went near the shaft again, but the fright he had experienced wore off quickly. The next time he decided to make a horizontal exploration to find the limits of the cave dimension. He pressed himself through a narrow crevice in the granite toward a faint light. As he came to the end of the fissure, he saw daylight and mist through the opening and emerged expecting to see Huashan.

Instead he saw a forest stretching to the horizon. Confused, he tried to orient himself. As best as he could calculate, there was no forest in that direction. And even if there had been a place he had somehow never seen, it was impossible for such a wide expanse to exist anywhere around the Huashan range.

He was reluctant to venture too far away from the cave, so he carefully gazed at and examined the scene. The trees were primarily thick, gnarled pines. There were no broadleaf trees, and this gave the forest a primeval quality. No bird raised a song, nor was there the sound of wind or stream. The ancient forest was completely still.

Saihung returned to the crevice and made his way back to his chambers. He noted everything in his diary and later questioned the Grand Master. He had seen the Forest of Infinity, said his master. No one had seen its end. Even the realized masters did not venture there, for once a person lost his way he could never return.

On another afternoon, Saihung chanced on an opening he had never seen before. It was high up on the wall of a narrow cavern. He climbed up to the opening and onto a sunlit ledge. The rock shelf was a small indentation in the sheer cliff face, wide enough for Saihung to stretch out and enjoy the warmth of the late afternoon. Across a plunging crevice he saw another cliff topped by forests. He relaxed and gazed appreciatively at the lush scenery.

In a moment, an animal appeared and began prancing before him. It was about the size and shape of a pony but it was unlike any other creature Saihung had ever seen. Although it had hooves and a body shaped like a pony, it had a deer's head, a fluffy tail, and scales on its body. Excitedly, it pranced and circled, stood on its hind legs, pawed the dirt, and whinnied like a horse, all in apparent urging for Saihung to come and join it. But Saihung could do nothing. The chasm made it impossible for the two to meet. The animal left periodically, only to peek out coyly from behind a tree and rush forth to frolic again before him.

Saihung watched the animal's dance until the sun began to set. He turned to begin his evening practices. The animal

seemed disappointed and stood sadly at the cliff's edge. Saihung turned for one last look. It seemed so beautiful as it
tossed its head slowly in the flaming light.

At the next weekly visit from his master, Saihung asked him
about the animal.

"*Da Shi,* I am beginning to see unusual creatures. Two days
ago, I saw an odd pony, and today I saw a rabbit."

Saihung described the animal. His master replied tersely.

"That scene and everything you experience is something
meant for you. It's up to you to try and understand the meaning yourself."

"At least the animal was there, but the rabbit was even more
strange."

"What happened?"

"I regularly go through a grotto that has grass on its floor.
Today I was startled to see a ring of mushrooms and a rabbit. I
went through the grotto and returned less than five minutes
later. Both the rabbit and mushrooms were gone. Could the
rabbit have eaten the mushrooms? Even if it had, there should
have been holes in the grass, or chewed off stalks. Instead the
grass was completely intact."

"Perhaps the gods are sending you a sign," said the Grand
Master.

"But what does the sign mean?"

"Find out yourself. If you can't do it, ask the gods yourself,
in your dream state."

Six months of practice had elapsed and Saihung, writing in
his diary, tried continually to assess his experiences. He now
genuinely enjoyed meditation. He laughed in amusement.
Huashan had trained him for a decade before he had reached
that point. Now the serenity, the joy, the feeling of absolute
health, and the thrill of learning had literally become addict-
ing.

There was no boredom. Meditation had made him sensitive.
Far from missing human beings, he relished the solitude. His

senses and feelings had become so sharpened that there was more than enough stimulation. Art and music were diversion enough. Self-discovery was learning enough. And his unusual experiences, real or visionary, were wondrous enough.

Saihung puzzled over his experiences. They were riddles, enigmas to him. Were the shaft, the Forest of Infinity, the pony, and the rabbit real or hallucinations? Had he only seen these things out of madness? Or did they exist with or without his perception? Perhaps it was only his point of view that was wrong. Perhaps his assumptions about reality were wrong. The sutras always emphasized that different things were illusory. Realities coexisted. Dimensions could interface at any place or time. Maybe everything existed at once. Or maybe the pony was real and the world of people wasn't.

Yet he had no doubt that he could have been lost down the shaft or in the forest, or fallen into the chasm. He continued to wonder whether these things existed independently or whether they were merely projections of his own psyche. In the months ahead, he experienced events so powerful that the question became more and more indistinct. No matter where the source of reality lay, he knew that it could affect him physically, mentally, and spiritually.

TWENTY-SEVEN

Temptation and Knowledge

WHEN SAIHUNG entered the cave, he expected to be there for nine months. But nine months had long since passed, and he had stopped inquiring about leaving. The Grand Master's response was always monotonously the same.

"Not yet. You haven't completed your task."

His master's weekly visits fortified him with contrasting guidance: the imparting of the sages' knowledge and the consistent dictum to face things alone. The Grand Master introduced Saihung to the *Tao Te Ching*, the *Jade Pivot*, the *Yellow Court Canon*, the *Tea Classic*, and deeper meditation techniques, but urged Saihung to confront his inner self constantly with his own resources. He instructed Saihung to remain open to mystical experiences that might come to him, but to distinguish between those that could impart true knowledge to him and those that could disrupt his progress.

The Grand Master often reminded Saihung of what was at stake. Saihung knew of some men confined to cells for life because they had been driven insane by the strain of the cave—whether they had lost their mental balance from loneliness, mistakes in meditation, or from some outside source was difficult to say. Others had committed suicide. Some had become lost in the maze of tunnels. But the Grand Master encouraged Saihung by saying that those who succeeded emerged with unshakable faith.

One and a half years had passed calmly. Saihung even had regular companions now. He fed birds with rice saved from his meals, and he had also befriended a monkey who traded fruit for portions of Saihung's dinners. The two became very close and the monkey periodically sat on Saihung's broad shoulders to ritually pick nonexistent lice from Saihung's hair. Nothing more unusual happened until Saihung one day looked up from his meditation platform and noticed the pool. There was a man's head in the water looking at him.

The face with long, wet, and uncombed hair and beard, was what the Taoist physiognomists called a "yin-yang face." One side of it was greenish, and the eye was large, black, and round. The other side was human, but with a bitter look to it. A yin-yang face meant the creature was originally an animal who, by practicing supernatural methods, had succeeded in evolving into human form. But no creature could completely forsake its old form. Something had to remain, and the left side seemed definitely reptilian. But it might be an apparition after all, Saihung told himself. The face stared at him unblinkingly. Stubborn and not to be intimidated by what was probably only an illusion, Saihung glared back obstinately.

"*I* am the resident of this grotto," said the head. "What are *you* doing here?"

"I am an ascetic practicing austerities," replied Saihung.

"How could you be practicing austerities? You're just a kid. You can't know very much. I have been cultivating myself for five hundred years and have five hundred more years to go."

"Oh, stop pretending!" shouted Saihung. "Stop it or I'll squash you with one kick!"

The head's eyes opened wide in surprise. Saihung saw the naked man leap from the water onto a rock in one movement. His body was short and thin, with dangling arms and long fingers. His hair hung to his knees.

The man stood laughing. Saihung was taken aback at the man's nakedness, and the man noticed right away. He turned a circle and was instantly clothed in Taoist robes. He giggled.

"I am the Toad Taoist," he announced. "Who are you?"

"I am Kwan Saihung, Zhengyi sect of Huashan."

"Zhengyi sect, eh? Who's your master?"

"The Grand Master of Huashan."

"I know him," laughed the Toad Taoist. "He's a silly old

fool. Why don't you give up this nonsense?"

"Why don't you shut up? You're not even real!"

The Toad Taoist went into a fit of laughter. Saihung decided to ignore him, and began his sutra recitation. The Toad Taoist jeered at him, laughed at him, and insulted him for four hours. He had no shortage of breath, and the walls of the rock chamber resounded with his heckling.

Eventually, when he saw that Saihung wasn't to be provoked, he gradually subsided. When Saihung completed his last recitation, the Toad Taoist addressed him in a somewhat more conciliatory tone.

"All right. No one meets me unless they're destined to. What do you want?"

"Nothing."

This set the Toad Taoist laughing again and he leapt froglike over the pool, landing right before Saihung. Saihung stood up. The Toad Taoist rushed up behind him and stood mimicking Saihung's stance. Saihung stepped to the left. So did he. Saihung walked in a circle. The man shadowed him exactly. Wherever Saihung walked, the Toad Taoist duplicated his very move. Saihung looked back in exasperation. The Toad Taoist grinned and looked at him with an insane expression.

Saihung sat down. The Toad Taoist leaned over Saihung's shoulder and rolled his eyes up at him. After a minute more, he spoke again.

"You're an all right kid, I'll admit," said the Toad Taoist as he sat down. "There is some substance to the Zhengyi sect after all. Listen, my boy, do you know why I'm here?"

"No."

"Centuries ago I got into a big fight, and as punishment I was sentenced to this grotto for a thousand years. Well, I'm halfway through now, but I am still cultivating myself continuously. Now what about you? What are you practicing?"

"I am practicing Taoist alchemy and meditation."

"Is that so?" said the Toad Taoist thoughtfully. "Then you must meditate on the *ling qiu.*"

The Toad Taoist

"Yes, I do."

"As I said earlier, no one meets me unless the stars decree it. You must have been destined to meet me. I should tell you something as a gift.

"You must realize that, as a student of Taoist alchemy, the *ling qiu* meditation is essential to your progress. But did you know that those psychic centers don't exist? They're only patterns that you imagine at a certain place in your body, imagined patterns that activate the subconscious and release power. In actuality, it is not some psychic center, but purely the mind. Do you realize what I'm saying? The mind is everything. Everything!"

He walked up to Saihung and in a smooth movement brought his palm before Saihung's face.

"Here's a bowl," he said, "and some fruit. An orange, grapes, peaches. This is the power of the *ling qiu!*"

Saihung tried to think carefully. He touched the fruit. They were real. But he was suspicious. Perhaps the Toad Taoist was presenting him with a puzzle. He thought back and realized that the preceding few moments had been blocked from his consciousness. Fleeting images of the Toad Taoist bending down came to him.

"Those grapes are a twig," said Saihung. Instantly, the grapes reverted. "That orange is a rock. The other fruit are leaves. The bowl is a flat stone." As he mentioned each item, it changed back to its original state and fell from the Toad Taoist's hand.

"I'll admit you're intelligent," said the Toad Taoist smiling broadly. "You can see how powerful the mind is. You could have eaten that fruit. But would you have been eating a rock or a fruit? The mind decides that. Take the cave itself. We agree this cave exists. It wouldn't if our minds willed otherwise. But what does it matter? The *ling qiu* don't exist and yet they work!"

The Toad Taoist floated into the air.

"I am using the *dan tian* combined with the throat center," he said. "How can I do it if the *ling qiu* don't exist? It is the mind. I tell you, nothing is real, nothing exists except the mind."

He instructed Saihung in deeper *ling qiu* meditation before saying goodbye. The Toad Taoist jumped into the water and slowly sank until just his head bobbed at the surface. Then that too sank until he was gone. He would return to visit Saihung regularly, but he always arrived and departed in the same odd way.

"Remember, my boy," he called just before he submerged completely. "Nothing is real!"

One day, Saihung, leaving the chamber, crossed a large stone bridge that vaulted the stream. He noticed an old man and an old woman at the other end. They were dressed in country clothes. The man's snowy hair was put up in a topknot, and he carried a long pipe. The woman had white hair that hung down to her heels, and she carried a straw broom. They greeted him.

"We are bamboo trees over two thousand years old."

"Two-thousand-year-old trees are possible," said Saihung, "but bamboos cannot be people."

"I see by your clothes and talisman that you're a Taoist," said the woman. "You should know such things are possible."

"Anything that is ancient," explained the man, "can be anything it wants. Things need not remain fixed. Take you, for example. You're an ordinary human being. How long could you live? A hundred years? A hundred and fifty? You don't understand the powers of ancient beings."

"You're a Taoist," smiled the woman, "and we know all Taoists seek immortality. We can confer immortality on you, and you can see for yourself the power of ancient things. You will have abilities to do things you cannot even imagine now."

"Nothing is free," said Saihung. "What do you want in return?"

"Ahh, a straightforward fellow!" exclaimed the old man,

"You would only have to be a bamboo for a short period in our service. We can transform your healthy body into a vigorous bamboo that would reproduce and cover the earth with bamboo forests. After you had propagated bamboo everywhere, you would not only be immortal but you would be able to fly, transform objects, become invisible, enter other dimensions—why, you'd rival the gods themselves! Follow us. Believe in us, and you'll become immortal."

"Thanks for the entertainment," said Saihung mockingly. "However, a person's life span is predestined. Longevity is a gift only from the gods, not something to be bargained for. I don't want your powers. They're only delusion."

The old man rushed forward with an angry roar and struck at him. Saihung warded off the blow and counterattacked, but the old man dodged his blows. The woman leapt on him, clawing at his face. Saihung jumped from the bridge and drew a talisman in the sand before him.

The infuriated man drew a deep inhalation from his pipe and blew a thick cloud of smoke toward him. His wife raised the broom to fan the vapor toward Saihung.

"You are demons!" shouted Saihung as he pointed at them. "I'll recite the Demon Catcher sutra!"

The old couple stopped in fright. Saihung recited the first line and they fled.

While crossing the same bridge three months later, Saihung noticed something hanging like a bat, but it was very large. Saihung looked closer. It was a boy.

As soon as he was noticed, the boy jumped down. He was grotesque. Barely four feet high, his face was pale, with narrow eyes, two prominent nostrils, and a mouth like a slit in rubber. When he began talking, Saihung noticed that he barely moved his lips, as if making an effort to hide his teeth.

As if to compensate for his ugliness the boy was dressed in a martial artist's costume so beautiful that it fascinated Saihung. He wore a silk brocade tunic and pants of peacock blue and

The Mysterious Child

white with black piping, sash, and bat, star, and flower designs. He wore a deep blue cape and jade beads with an opal amulet. In spite of himself, Saihung was quite taken with the boy's blue shoes embroidered in beautiful cloud designs.

"I want to play," said the boy in a squeaky voice. "Will you be my playmate?"

"Sorry, I have other things to do."

"Please! Please be my playmate. I know you like to play too. I know all the hiding places in the mountain. I can show you places no mortal has seen. I can give you treasures of which even heaven itself cannot conceive! Only please be my playmate!"

"Sorry, I can't play today."

The boy walked dejectedly to a rock and sat down. Putting his face into his hands he began to sob. "You don't know! You can't understand how lonely I am. It's not very much fun in this cave. Sometimes no one comes for decades. I've been here for centuries—can't you imagine how lonely it must be?"

Saihung stood up to leave.

"Wait! Wait! Don't you like martial arts?"

Saihung was immediately interested.

"Look!" The boy did a dazzling set in a style Saihung had never seen. He had to admit it was impressive. The boy's palm techniques rivaled the Grand Master's, and his flips and acrobatic tactics were close to flying.

"Whatever martial art you like, I know it!" continued the boy when he concluded his performance. "Be my companion and you'll be an unrivaled martial hero. You need never fear. I'll always protect you. I can see evil, even in the dark. Join me, and we will be friends and have fun forever."

"Suppose I'm interested?"

"We'll be playmates for eternity!" said the boy, clapping his hands in delight. "But there is a problem. You're a mortal. Here. Eat this honeyed apple and you will be immortal."

"No, thanks."

The boy frowned.

"How about this?" he proposed after a few minutes. "Let's

have a match. If I win, you eat the apple and become my play-mate. If I lose, I'll never bother you again."

He held out the apple. Saihung kicked it from his hand.

"Ohhh, you shouldn't have done that," growled the boy. "When I ask someone to be my friend, he becomes my friend or I subtract him from the world!"

The boy leapt at him, and Saihung found the boy's skill superior. He could not even return a blow. Wherever he turned, a palm came slicing down. His every kick was blocked and countered with one of the boy's own acrobatic kicks.

"You'd better eat the apple now," said the boy as he applied an arm lock. "What's so bad about it anyway? You'll be immortal."

Saihung freed himself with a mighty back kick. The boy charged, and Saihung reached into his robes for his *Ba Gua* mirror. He held it before him. The boy screamed, covered his face, and fled.

Saihung was still in a cold sweat when he went back to his chambers. He washed himself and prepared for bed. He heard a low tone, a soft buzzing that he had heard on many previous nights.

"Sometime I'll have to find out what that buzzing is all about," he said to himself.

That opportunity soon came. Saihung found an entrance to a grotto, revealed because the stream had receded. Here the buzzing was louder. He swam across the stream and found a tunnel that went steeply upward. He crawled up for twenty-five feet to a small spherical grotto. A glow illuminated the chamber. Saihung saw that an enormous root hanging from the ceiling emitted both the light and the buzzing.

The root was buff colored, with many branches as fine as hair. Saihung examined it. It was vibrating, and the buzzing sounded like religious chanting.

"Excuse me," Saihung addressed the root. "What kind of being are you?"

"I am a ginseng root, and I'm so lucky that you've come by," replied a female voice. "I've been here for a thousand years. My roots have grown painfully long. Down below, I hurt hanging like this. Up above, the birds try to eat me. So far, my leaves and branches have protected me, but now they are being devoured by insects. If you don't rescue me, I'll surely be lost."

"But how can I rescue you?" asked Saihung. "You are growing through the very rock of Huashan. You have so many slender roots that I'm afraid I'd break them."

"If you're willing to rescue me, nothing is impossible. Rock is hard only because you don't understand it. In fact, it has a grain and hundreds of hairline cracks. Take up a stick and a rock. Strike where I tell you."

Saihung followed her instructions, chiseling for over two hours. The rock, to his surprise, crumbled swiftly away. It was easy with the root directing him to the weak points of the stone. When Saihung had hollowed enough of a hole, he gently pulled down the root, leaving her leaves and branches above, and wrapped her in a cloth.

"Thank you! Thank you!" said the root in relief. "Please don't let the sun hit me. I'll dry out."

Saihung took her into the cool darkness of his chambers before he unwrapped her.

"Ginseng is one of the most life-giving of herbs," said the root in a melodious voice. "You saved my life, and now I am committed to you. I know that Taoists want immortality. If you place me on your head as you enter meditation, I'll grow into you. Our lives will sustain one another for eternity."

"A plant's nature is immobility." Saihung responded. "I am a man. If I accepted your offer, I could never move again."

"But you'd be immortal."

"You aren't human. I am. You can't understand that I have no desire for immobility. Trees live for thousands of years, and, yes, they are alive, but they cannot move."

"What a waste," sighed the root.

"Perhaps not," said Saihung menacingly. "I could eat you."

The root trembled.

"I'm a living being," cried the root. "Don't eat me. I know Taoists are sworn not to take life. You can't kill me! It's better to accept my offer. We'll live together forever."

"I'm sorry, but I have my own quest. My time is almost up. My teacher should be coming soon. If he finds you, I'm sure he won't hesitate to eat you."

"Who is your teacher?" asked the root cautiously.

"The Grand Master of Huashan."

"What? Is that old fox still around?"

"Oh, yes, and I seem to recall that he mentioned misplacing a ginseng root somewhere. I'm going to tell him where you are!"

"No! No! Please free me! I'll tell you things I've seen in the past thousand years. I'll tell you about herbal medicine. But spare me, please."

Saihung agreed, and they spent the rest of the night in conversation. In the morning he found an open grotto with rich soil, abundant light, and a tiny spring, where he planted her. He returned from time to time to water her and watched with pleasure as she sprouted new leaves.

Saihung sat comfortably on the meditation platform reading his evening sutra. He had almost memorized the entire scripture in the two years he had been in the cave. The oil lamp burned brightly, and he was almost completely immersed in his contemplation when something caught his eye. On the opposite bank was a young woman with a basket. She was a willowy figure, dressed in a peach-colored silk gown and a diaphanous cape. Her presence was a rich contrast to the roughness of the cave. Saihung looked more closely at her face. She had large brown eyes that radiated a hypnotic feline quality. Her skin was as smooth as satin, and the trace of blush on her cheeks was a fainter echo of her full red lips. Her lustrous black hair, perfectly coiffed, was like a cloud pinned with gold.

Seeing Saihung, she placed her basket aside and shyly pulled a rose-colored scarf from her sleeve. Veiling her nose and mouth, she stood at the water's edge.

"Oh, sir!" she cried out. "How fortunate I am to have met you. I'm afraid I've lost my way."

Saihung looked at her in alarm. He put his hands into a protective prayer gesture. She paused almost imperceptibly when he did that.

"Oh, sir! Won't you please help me?" she repeated.

Saihung recited a sutra for protection. The woman stepped back.

"Why recite that?" she asked in a hurt tone. "There's no need. I won't harm you. Here, I'll entertain you with a dance. Perhaps that will reassure you that I'm only an innocent girl."

Singing in a high, clear voice, she began a graceful dance. Her every note was perfect, her movements flawless. She seemed to be the very embodiment of femininity. When she finished her dance with a gentle bow, however, she saw that Saihung was immobile and still reciting.

"Ahh, you're an ascetic, I see," she said. "If that's what you're interested in, let me tell you that I have achieved power far beyond what you can ever hope for with all this dreary sitting. I can control the Five Elements. I can command wind and rain. Limitless wealth is mine at any moment. I have everlasting youth and beauty. And I enjoy the boundless pleasures of love.

"Doesn't that far surpass your tradition? A Taoist remains poor, and even if he manages to acquire immortality, he loses beauty and youth. Your tradition also includes celibacy, believing that abstinence will maintain vitality. But I, far from weakening with love, become stronger—as do my lovers.

"Look at yourself. You're muscular, strong, and handsome. It's obvious that it isn't your destiny to remain a begging, ash-covered monk with matted hair, but to become a great prince instead. Come with me. Be my lover. Not only will you know for the first time the pleasure of a woman's love, but you shall

The Peach Maiden

gain powers far surpassing your master's."

Saihung continued reciting. The woman sighed.

"Why put on this silly show, sir? Don't you believe me? Or are you the type who only believes what he sees?"

Saihung broke into a sweat from the effort of recitation. He tried to bring his resolution to the fore as he apprehensively watched the woman.

She turned away from him, unpinning her hair. It fell in a dark, heavy cascade. As if the cloud of her hair had burst and rained perfume, Saihung breathed in an exciting fragrance. She turned toward him and slowly removed her cape and outer robes until she stood only in her underrobe. Never taking her eyes from his, she slowly undid its ties. Saihung saw the translucent skin at her neck sweep downward into an expanse of warm nakedness.

Her body was perfect. From the soft slope of her shoulders to her full breasts, over her slender hips, down to her long, shapely legs, she could have been made of jade and gold. She used her flowing hair to veil herself, but it was the contrast between that curtain and what lay boldly open to Saihung's gaze that made the dance of her limbs the most maddening.

"They tell me," she said breathlessly, "that men desire all kinds of women. What woman do you crave in your innermost fantasy? What woman makes your loins blaze with want? I can be that woman. I can fulfill your every fantasy. Look!"

She transformed herself into a Hindu woman. Almond-shaped eyes were like onyx and ivory set in the lush amber of her skin. Her breasts were heavy with desire.

"Or do you prefer this?" she asked as she changed into a Persian woman with long hair and a full figure. Her flesh was like alabaster, and her movements were a seductive play of light and shadow.

"They say that all Chinese men crave Hindu and Persian women the most because of their great erotic skill," she said, changing back to her original form. "I know all styles of love. Come and embrace me. Embrace eternal youth. Love me.

You'll be a prince of the greatest stature. Take me. You'll command magnificent powers. Possess me. I'll be yours for eternity. Enter me. Love me over and over. You'll feel as if you are loving a woman with constant virginal purity; yet I'll use my maximum skill. I'll bring you pleasure that will burn, consume, satisfy your innermost hungers, and still arouse a passion that will leave you ever eager for the infinite variations of love."

Saihung sat in stony stiffness, hands pressed together, lips reciting endlessly.

The woman grew angry when she saw that he was not to be moved.

"How dare you scorn me!" she shouted. "No man does that. You stupid monk. You sit there mumbling inanities while the ultimate in the world's riches, powers, and pleasures is yours for the taking! All that idiotic chanting will get you nowhere—and it certainly won't defend you."

She whirled in a circular dance, and where she once stood as a voluptuous nude, there was now only an eerie, trembling pillar of long green hair. It shook frighteningly, emitting a loud cackling that echoed sharply in the cavern.

The pillar revolved slowly and Saihung saw the woman's face at the top. Her face began to elongate as it turned green. The eyes expanded into black orbs. The hair became a smooth scaly skin. Legs appeared. She metamorphosed into a six-foot lizard.

The lizard slithered into the pool and swam across. Rearing up before the sacred circle, she hissed loudly and flicked her tongue. But though she lunged terrifyingly at him, she couldn't penetrate the power of his sutra.

Saihung was miserable with fear. His hands were wet with perspiration, his robes were soaked. He recited continually. To break his sutra was to lose everything.

The lizard disappeared abruptly, and all was temporarily quiet until a dot appeared in the sublime darkness. It expanded into her face. The once beautiful visage was now a cruelly laughing woman; her soft hair now writhed like snakes around her. She darted at him. Each time she reached the perimeter of the circle he felt a blow in the pit of his stomach. His body broke into a fever as she maintained the attacks for an hour. Mournful sniffing sounds and pitiful wailing filled the air. He was close to nausea.

She disappeared. He did not dare stop reciting. A howling wind blew on him, extinguishing the torches, and knocking over his oil lamp. The glass broke, and the oil flashed into an uncontrolled fire.

A darting flame rose and sped around the cave like a bat on fire. It fluttered maddeningly around him and struck his psychic shield repeatedly. He noticed that her attacks had now penetrated the sacred circle and were closing in. He was hysterical and almost on the verge of tears.

The flame exploded before him and her face was there once again, her hair rooting itself into the nocturnal air. She laughed mockingly and opened her mouth. She edged toward him and the mouth grew in size. She would devour him.

Saihung heard the temple bells almost inaudibly; dawn was coming. She pressed toward him. He could feel her hot breath, as her lips and teeth opened.

A ray of light edged through the rim of one of the skylights and struck her face. She retreated and reappeared in the beautiful form that she first had come to him. The grotto brightened, and she faded with a moan.

Saihung stopped chanting only when it was definitely day. He stood up in relief. His arms ached and his legs were stiff. He looked down in sudden awareness. Embarrassed, he realized that he had been so frightened that he had wet his pants.

He took off his clothes and dived into the pool. On the far end, he saw a nose rising. It was the Toad Taoist.

"I see that she tried to get you," he said as he swam over.

Saihung nodded, smiling at the thought that he had overcome the ordeal. The Toad Taoist giggled, splashed him, and spat water at him.

"You have a strong mind," congratulated the Toad Taoist as he dunked Saihung. "That's good. Someday there will be a crisis involving the whole world. It will be a confrontation between good and evil. You'll need this strength to survive."

TWENTY-EIGHT

Internal Gazing

SAIHUNG LOOKED within his body. It was transparent.

Meditation, after all, was not stillness. The body always moved: the heart pumped, blood flowed, electricity fired the nerves, energy coursed through the meridians, the organs pulsated in concert, and the lungs, even if they slowed to an apparent stop, still breathed on in an exaggerated timeline. The human being never stopped moving, never stopped changing. A human being was a cosmos. A mysterious progression. A sacred equilibrium.

Saihung looked deeply into himself. He was completely immersed in that which was inner. Inner became everything. Inside and outside became one. Plunging deep within, he came to the perfect realization. Inner and outer became one in infinity.

He was a focus. A pinpoint in the cosmos. A place where infinity had congealed into one mass of movement and experience. Qi had become the Five Elements, had become Yin and Yang, had become a human being. He was a microcosm of eternity.

Saihung imagined the Big Dipper Constellation.

Silence. Space. Everything was real. Nothing was real. Both were equal. Time and space doubled back on each other in serpentine layers and lost their distinction. What went beyond duality?

The Big Dipper descended.

Humanity was a microcosm of the universe. They were one. One was everything. The organs were planets. The psychic centers were novas. The meridian points were stars. The meridians were pathways to heaven.

The Big Dipper came to him. He called it. He willed it.

He entered it, and it lifted him past the highest clouds, through the sleek canopy of the azure sky into blackness. All was dark save the scatter of stars. The universe was night, but day exploded and burned in its folds.

He hung there floating. It was soundless. He had projected the stars into himself and now he himself was projected like a star. He was a body in space. Like a planet. A meteor. A sun.

But there was a deeper state. He still was a body. Why was it here, but not over there?

His body expanded in a silent explosion. His perfect mechanism unwound and shot itself in a thousand directions. The body was gone, but an intention still lingered. A memory, distant and shimmering—a strange streak of individualism still floating in space.

The streak dissipated. Beyond stars, planets, and dimensions, beyond any kaleidoscope of reality, piercing infinite layers. Gone. There was only Nothingness.

Saihung sat in the cavern. He felt small. Humble. He was the speck that was everything and nothing.

Solitude and contemplation were all he wanted. Why had he had to return? The gods had willed it. He had a task, and until he fulfilled it he was in bondage on the earth. But the gods had let him glimpse the other side. He had seen it. He would have stayed, had he not been returned.

He didn't want to be here. Nothing on earth was real. What passed for civilization, that supposed massive cultural search for perfection, was only the glorification of grotesque human narcissism. What passed for emotion was only the visceral exercise of perversion. Nothing beckoned to him.

He sat in stillness. He knew he had a task. He was put here for it. Something glimmered in him like a childhood memory. It was compassion: he had been returned not only for his own quest but to help others.

He heard a sound. He saw a moving torch. It was his master.

"It's time for you to leave." The Grand Master smiled as he

placed a gentle hand on Saihung's shoulder.

He blindfolded Saihung to protect his eyes from the sunlight and led him to an enclosed shrine. Saihung soaked in herbal baths to cleanse his skin, which had turned blue from living in the earth and bathing in mineral waters. He put an herbal solution in his eyes to strengthen them. Gradually, over the course of a month he and the Grand Master widened a skylight. But Saihung could only see blue through it.

The day came for him to emerge. He heard his master break the seal and enter. In the semidarkness of the hut, Saihung knelt down before the Grand Master.

"You have been tested thoroughly. You have made great strivings. Only today do you finally glimpse what it is to be a Taoist.

"All that matters to a Taoist is that one is in harmony with nature. In one's character, one is like heaven and earth, as bright as the sun and the moon, as orderly as the four seasons.

"When one has attained Tao, one can even precede heaven, but heaven will not act in opposition, for one will act only as heaven would have at the time. One is not destroyed because one harmoniously follows only the cyclic motion of the Tao, avoiding the aggressive, extravagant expenditures of energy. Efforts to achieve strength and power may lead to short-term success, but such excessiveness ultimately results in an early death.

"The *Tao Te Ching* clearly states that when things reach the pinnacle of their strength, they begin to grow old. Therefore, excessive strength is contrary to Tao, and what is contrary to Tao will come to a speedy end.

"Thus one seeks not to build up one's own power, but to unite with Tao. One is not aggressive and mighty, but rather humble and peaceful. One seeks not to go the way of other men but rather to follow the cycles of nature. Only then can one know renewal and rejuvenation. Through returning and going forth, expansion and contraction, one knows infinity and perhaps even immortality. For at that point, one is wholly integrated with the Tao. One gives undivided attention to its vital energy, responding with the utmost pliancy. Then one can become like a newborn infant."

The Grand Master opened the door. A crack of light expanded into complete brightness. Saihung went into the light of a new world.

Author's Note

I HAD HEARD, through two friends, of a sixty-five-year-old martial arts teacher known only as "Mr. Kwan." They asked me if I had ever heard of him. I had not. But they were then searching for a teacher, and I accompanied them to visit his class. I had been involved in Chinese martial arts for five years and went to see if he was a genuine teacher.

We arrived early at the secluded park where he taught. The training area was empty. We went to another section to practice while we waited, and had become deeply engaged in Taiji pushing hands when a rather large man appeared in the bushes.

He looked about thirty years old and had medium-long black hair and enormously heavy shoulders. Dressed in a gray sweatshirt and brown warm-up suit, he stood completely motionless and stared unabashedly at us. I was annoyed.

He looked like a college student, a jock out to provoke people. If he were a student of Mr. Kwan's, why didn't he go and wait respectfully for his master instead of lurking about? He disappeared, and a few minutes later one of Mr. Kwan's students came to tell us that the teacher had arrived. As we walked down the hill, she warned us that her teacher was an excellent one, but very traditional and "very eccentric."

The class was practicing *qigong* when we arrived. I was instantly impressed by the vigor and variety of the movements. The postures were forceful, yet balanced. But to my surprise, the man from the bushes was leading the class.

I turned to the student. "Is that the senior student?" I asked.

"No, that's Mr. Kwan," she replied.

"I thought he was in his mid-sixties."

"He is."

I looked closely at him. Mr. Kwan had only a very slight bit of gray hair, and one had to look quite carefully to see it. His wide face was smooth-skinned and clear, and he had large, luminescent eyes that demonstrated a sensitive awareness of his surroundings. This man was the furthest thing possible from the stereotype of an old, wizened teacher.

At a break in the class, we were formally introduced. Mr. Kwan proved to be rather shy, and after greeting us he retreated to watch his students. Toward the end of class, reassured by his students that he was approachable, I went to speak with him. In particular I wanted to know who his teachers had been.

In the Asian tradition, a teacher is only as good as the lineage of his school. When I questioned him about his, I was stunned to learn that some of his teachers were among the most famous in China. He said he had trained with such masters as Yang Cheng fu and Chen Weiming of Taiji, Sun Lutang of Xingyi, Fu Zhensong and Zhang Zhaodong of Bagua, as well as Wang Zeping of Mizhongyi. It was not until later that I found out that Mr. Kwan had studied a large number of other martial styles, including Shaolin, Taoist, Monkey, Eagle, Crane, Snake, and Tiger forms. I also learned subsequently that Mr. Kwan had traveled all over the world, had gone to India and Tibet to study yoga and other meditative systems, had been a soldier, a circus performer, Peking Opera performer, Beijing University political science teacher, and under secretary to Zhou Enlai.

His martial background attracted me. Most present-day masters have studied only with students of these famous teachers, and yet here was a man who represented the first generation taught by those masters. Eager to study with him, I inquired about the tuition.

Mr. Kwan looked visibly embarrassed. Money matters seemed to make him uncomfortable. He hesitantly told me that it was $35 a month. There was a pause. He added that for this sum, a student could train with him four or five times a week, if desired. There was another pause. As if he felt the cost was still insufficiently justified, he went on to explain what the money was to be used for.

Out of the $35, only $10 went to sustain himself. Another $10 was set aside for the future building of a school, and the remaining $15 was sent back to China to support his master.

I asked which master it was. All the masters he had named had passed away, and I tried to imagine what kind of master this man could have.

"My Taoist master," replied Mr. Kwan.

"Your Taoist master?" I was excited. I had originally entered martial arts in the hopes of finding a man such as Mr. Kwan. It was said that the spiritual could be reached through martial training, and while I had trained in Taijiquan with several successive teachers, I had never found anyone who might have instructed me fully. I was still searching for a master who could teach me both martial arts and philosophy.

"He must be very old," I said, trying to keep the subject going. Mr. Kwan was quiet, reluctant to discuss his master.

"He is," Mr. Kwan said after a moment of decision. "He has long white hair and beard and is now 142 years old. He spends his time in meditation."

"142! Is that possible?"

"Of course. He's a Taoist."

"And you?"

"I am also a Taoist ascetic. In fact, I only teach martial art as a sideline."

We talked for a while more until Mr. Kwan had to leave. I returned to visit his class several times, and soon became his student. I was as interested in the rare and orthodox martial arts he taught as in his Taoism. I liked being his student and addressed him as *Sifu*.

I had seemingly endless doubt and uncertainty, which I put to Sifu in question after question. He usually gave profound answers, yet in a way that made complete sense. But some-

238 | AUTHOR'S NOTE

times he would only tell me that I had to face the problem alone. This never seemed to be an attempt to avoid an issue he couldn't discuss. Although he was generous with his guidance, he always placed squarely on me the responsibility for my own life.

I had read many books on Taoism, but as my relationship with Sifu deepened, I found that his Taoism was a complete and living tradition that went beyond theoretical book knowledge. Taoism, for Sifu, was more than a religion or a philosophy. It was a way of life. At its very core, this Taoism was the discipline of natural living and complete self-purification for the sake of spiritual advancement. Thus, although the Taoist tradition encompassed sorcery, ritual, and religious belief in an enormous pantheon, Sifu's emphasis was on ascetic practice to gain liberation from ignorance and sorrow.

Toward this goal, he of course spoke of the appreciation of nature and the noncontentious outlook about which I had often read. But his basic theme was self-sacrifice to achieve purification and perfection. This meant the seemingly simple task of avoiding degradation of ourselves, of our bodies, of others, or of the world around us.

"The gods have a test for us to take," Sifu said. "Whether we want to or not, they will test our willingness to sacrifice and reach the other side of enlightenment instead of succumbing to greed and our own degradation. The body is the temple of God, the soul is God himself. If you pollute your own body and it deteriorates, and your brain disintegrates, God will naturally leave your body. But if you know enough to sacrifice, you will reach a certain rewarding stage. Then you'll give up all that is 'nice,' easy to get, and 'fun,' and you'll eventually purify your body. That is like cleaning and repainting a temple to await God's entrance."

The avoidance of degradation meant a regulated diet, no liquor, drugs, smoking, or sexual excess. City noise, air pollution, and stress were to be shunned. I found that Sifu himself was the best example. He was celibate, fastidious in his diet, neither smoked nor took drugs, drank a single glass of wine on rare occasions, trained daily, and, in spite of a rather gruff exterior, was caring and protective of his students.

He has been practicing for over five decades now, and he says he's still learning. Fortunately, he is willing to transmit his system to others. Although I can never have the privilege of membership in his sect, nor the opportunity to fully undertake asceticism and internal alchemy, I have still benefited enormously from his teaching. My health has improved; I have stopped numerous bad habits, including drugs and drinking; and I am happy in quiet and solitude. I appreciate life. That is why I feel that the simple concepts of nondegradation and working toward a natural equilibrium are healthy, nonsectarian views that anyone can adopt. Through that philosophy, it is possible to live in good health, be humble, dignified, and yet protect oneself from exploitation, abuse, and dehumanization. Living naturally and in harmony with the seasons, remaining involved in all the arts, and maintaining spiritual devotion can lead to salvation.

Many people wonder whether spirituality can exist in today's world. Warfare, nuclear disaster, pollution, crime, racism, social decay, sham religious leaders, and individual laziness all seem to make it impossible. Endless obstructions and diversions exist to discourage the practice of austerities. But Taoism is a methodical and gradual system. It is individually flexible and universally all-encompassing. Its approach from the physical to the spiritual implies that the religious can arise from the secular. One need only cultivate the right attitudes with sincerity.

It is unnecessary to withdraw from the world. The Taoists eschew withdrawal as irresponsible. The striving to live a pure, simple, and principled life is in itself Taoism. Sifu's own Taoism was transmitted at a time when China was in great turmoil. He learned to preserve his faith through war and secular society. He is proof that in the most difficult of times, one can still be spiritual.

He frequently recounts his own experiences in order to spur us on. He told how he had not been able to master the first move of Xingyi and had been teased by his class, and so he had simply omitted it from his practice until the teacher reprimanded him. He told us stories of his own matches, resulting both in victories and defeats. He spoke of his master's wisdom and strictness. And he told us entrancing stories of other old masters with abilities to go into other dimensions, perform sorcery, or match fighting skills against all challengers. Naturally, our curiosity soon extended into wondering about Sifu as an individual, and more about him than these parablelike tales revealed.

But Sifu was deliberately obscure whenever we probed into details of his personal past. A Taoist master is never to reveal his birthdate, birthplace, or other individual data. Yet, because we encountered a wide range of situations where he drew from his personal experiences to teach us, and because, like a father, he indulged us in answering some of our questions, Sifu slowly revealed parts of his past life.

The stories became an integral part of my early training, and I believe they will have value for others as well. This book may provide some idea of the struggles and rewards of a path, show the need for a good teacher, and describe seldom-seen teachings of Taoism. I hope that others, though knowing the difficulties, will find inspiration to undertake a spiritual path.